THE PLACE NAMES OF COUNTY DERRY

By
Brian Mitchell

Copyright © 2016
Brian Mitchell

ISBN 978-0-8063-5801-7

CLEARFIELD

Introduction

This book consists of two parts:

Part One: The Place Names of County Derry

This section contains a list of 1,750 place names, in alphabetical order, as recorded in the 1901 census returns for the city and county of Londonderry (also known as Derry). It includes the names of all townlands, together with street listings for all towns, in County Derry.

Against each place name, i.e. townland or town and street, is recorded the following information: District Electoral Division, Parish, Registrar District, Poor Law Union and 17th Century Landowner. Correct place name location – by D.E.D., Parish, Registrar District, Poor Law Union and Estate – will result in more effective use of major Irish record sources such as 1901 and 1911 census returns, church registers, civil registers of births, marriages and deaths, the national indexes to civil birth, marriage and death registers, and estate records.

Part Two: County Derry Parish Reports

Many record sources of value, both civil and church, to family historians were compiled and recorded by parish. By mid-19th century, County Derry was subdivided into 46 civil parishes. Realistic genealogical research, in the absence of indexes and databases, generally requires knowledge of the parish in which your ancestor lived.

This section details parish reports, in alphabetical order, for each of Derry's 46 civil parishes which describes and locates the parish, identifies the top ten surnames in mid-19th century and details the major record sources for that parish:

- Church Registers, their religious denomination and commencement dates
- Graveyards and their location in mid-19th century;
- Census Returns and Census Substitutes dating from 1663 to 1911.

The Place Names of County Derry

Part One

This is a list, in alphabetical order, of 1,750 place names as recorded in the 1901 census returns for the city and county of Londonderry (also known as Derry). It includes the names of all townlands, together with street listings for all towns, in County Derry.

Correct place name location – by District Electoral Division, Parish, Registrar District, Poor Law Union and Estate – will result in more effective use of major Irish record sources such as 1901 and 1911 census returns, church registers, civil registers of births, marriages and deaths, the national indexes to civil birth, marriage and death registers, and estate records.

Against each placename, i.e. townland or town and street, is recorded the following information:

Column Heading	Significance
D.E.D. Name	The 1901 and 1911 census returns were gathered by District Electoral Division. All placenames in County Derry were grouped into 83 District Electoral Divisions. **Tip to Researchers** – if you wish to examine families of interest in the vicinity of a townland of interest you should enter this name in 'DED' field when searching 1901 or 1911 census returns at www.census.nationalarchives.ie.
Parish	Many record sources of value, both civil and church, to family historians were compiled and recorded by parish. By mid-19th century, County Derry was subdivided into 46 civil parishes. **Tip to Researchers** – by using *A New Genealogical Atlas of Ireland* (2nd edition, Brian Mitchell, Genealogical Publishing Company, Baltimore, 2002) civil parish locations can be translated into Church of Ireland parishes, Roman Catholic parishes and Presbyterian Congregations; and by using *A Guide to Irish Parish Registers* (Brian Mitchell, Genealogical Publishing Company, Baltimore, 1988) civil parish locations can also be translated into a listing of surviving church registers of all denominations and their commencement dates.
Registrar District	Civil registration of births, deaths and Roman Catholic marriages in Ireland began on 1st January 1864 while non-Catholic marriages were subject to registration from 1st April 1845. For the purpose of civil registration, County Derry was divided into 24 local registrar districts, which were grouped into 4 poor law unions. Books recording births, marriages and deaths were kept in each local registrar district, and a consolidated name index, within each poor law union, was then compiled at national level.
Poor Law Union	County Derry was served by four poor law unions: Londonderry, Limavady (originally known as Newtownlimavady), Coleraine and Magherafelt. These districts, centred on a large market town, were created in 1838 for the financial support of the poor. Poor law unions were subdivided into Registration Districts (to gather civil birth, marriage and death details) which in turn were further subdivided into District Electoral Divisions (to gather census

	returns). **Tip to Researchers** – in the national indexes to civil birth, marriage and death registers the only clue to an address is the name of the Superintendent Registrar's District in which an event was registered. The Superintendent Registrar's District equates to the area served by the Poor Law Union.
17th Century Landowner	In 17th, 18th and 19th centuries, until they were finally broken up in the latter years of the 19th century under the Land Acts, the majority of the population of Ireland lived on large estates. The administration of these estates by landlords and their agents produced a large quantity of records, including maps, rentals, account books, leases, title deeds, surveys and other such matters. For example, rent rolls which list tenants on individual estates are a useful source of genealogical information. With the establishment of County Londonderry from 1613 the major landowners were the Church of Ireland and the Bishop of Derry; Sir Thomas Phillips, who first came to Ireland in 1599 with the English army; the twelve principal livery companies of the City of London, namely Clothworkers, Drapers, Fishmongers, Goldsmiths, Grocers, Haberdashers, Ironmongers, Mercers, Merchant Taylors, Salters, Skinners and Vintners; and the Irish Society, a company set up by the city of London to oversee the Plantation of Londonderry. Landownership evolved over time as freeholds were granted and as landlords sub-let or sold their estates to middlemen. The 'Immediate Lessors' column in Griffith's Valuation, at www.askaboutireland.ie/griffith-valuation, provides insight into landownership in the middle years of the 19th century. **Tip to Researchers** – once you know the name of your ancestor's landlord your next step will be to determine where the landowner's estate papers are deposited or if they are retained by the family. For example, estate papers for County Derry held in Public Record Office of Northern Ireland (www.proni.gov.uk) are listed, with description and reference details, in PRONI's *Guide to Landed Estate Records*.

Important:

If you can't find a placename you are looking for, there are two major reasons for this:

1. The place name you seek is spelt differently to the 'official' spelling. It is only in comparatively recent times, i.e. from mid-19th century, that attempts have been made to standardise the spelling of Irish placenames.

    Inconsistency in spelling of place names (and surnames) is well known to those who have conducted research into their Irish family history. An 'official' and standardised recording of townland names for all Ireland was established, by 1842, by the Ordnance Survey and published in maps at 6" to 1 mile and in the *Townland Index*.

    Place names, originally in Gaelic, were anglicised from the 17th century, by settlers with little knowledge of the Irish language. This resulted in a number of different spellings of the same place name. For example, in Clondermot Parish, County Derry, the townland which was standardised as Coolkeeragh in the Townland Index was recorded as Killkeeraugh in the 1831 census and as Culkeeragh in the Tithe Book of 1834.

2. Although the townland is the smallest and most ancient of Irish land divisions – there are 60,462 townlands in Ireland – and is effectively equated with identification of the ancestral home, it is quite possible that the place name you seek is even more localised than a townland name.

For example, Seoirse Ó Dochartaigh, a Gaelic-speaking musician, artist and genealogist of Mossyglen, Carndonagh (in *Inis Eoghain: The Island of Eoghan: The Place-Names of Inishowen*, published 2011) has identified 452 place names (many of them not recorded on any map) within the 30 'official' townlands and one island that make up the civil parish of Clonmany, County Donegal!

The Parishes Of County Londonderry

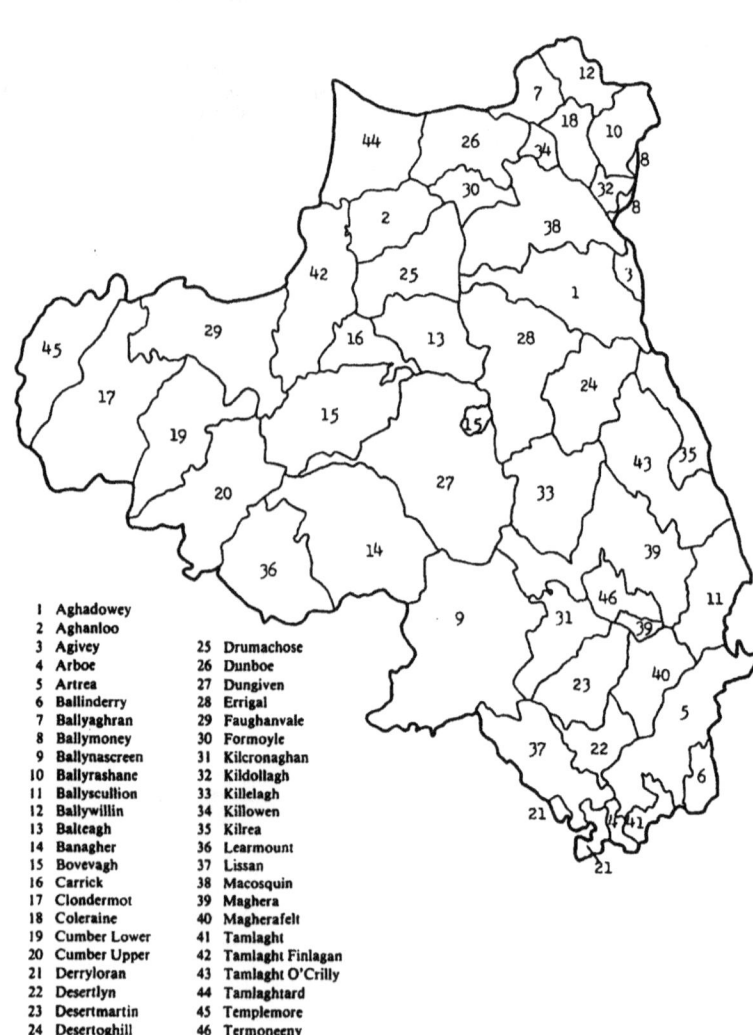

1 Aghadowey	
2 Aghanloo	
3 Agivey	25 Drumachose
4 Arboe	26 Dunboe
5 Artrea	27 Dungiven
6 Ballinderry	28 Errigal
7 Ballyaghran	29 Faughanvale
8 Ballymoney	30 Formoyle
9 Ballynascreen	31 Kilcronaghan
10 Ballyrashane	32 Kildollagh
11 Ballyscullion	33 Killelagh
12 Ballywillin	34 Killowen
13 Balteagh	35 Kilrea
14 Banagher	36 Learmount
15 Bovevagh	37 Lissan
16 Carrick	38 Macosquin
17 Clondermot	39 Maghera
18 Coleraine	40 Magherafelt
19 Cumber Lower	41 Tamlaght
20 Cumber Upper	42 Tamlaght Finlagan
21 Derryloran	43 Tamlaght O'Crilly
22 Desertlyn	44 Tamlaghtard
23 Desertmartin	45 Templemore
24 Desertoghill	46 Termoneeny

THE POOR LAW UNIONS OF COUNTY LONDONDERRY

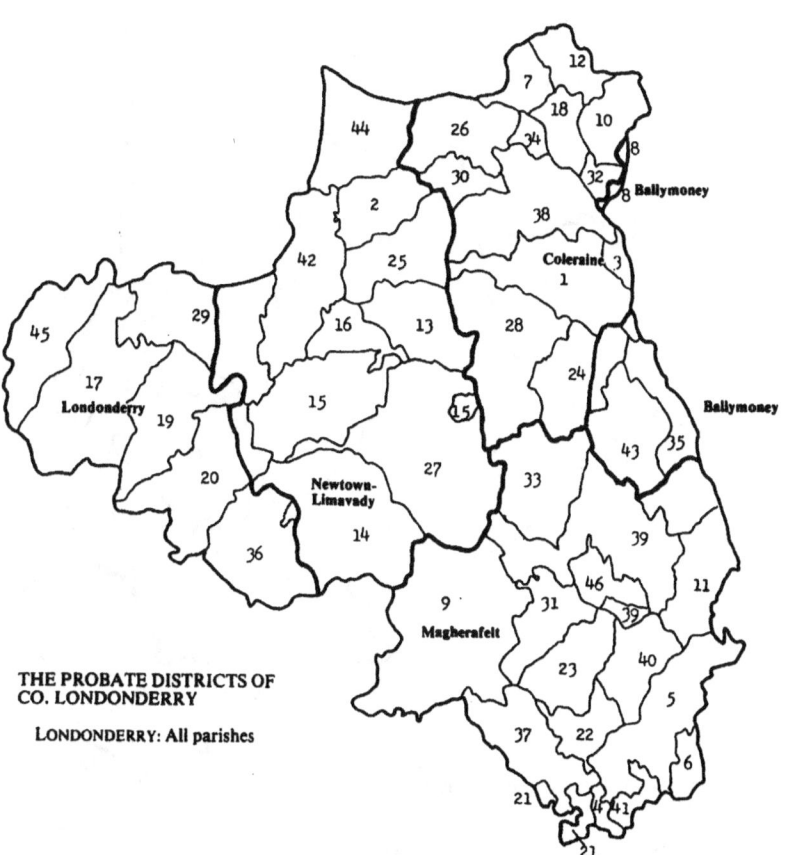

THE PROBATE DISTRICTS OF
CO. LONDONDERRY

LONDONDERRY: All parishes

THE ROMAN CATHOLIC PARISHES OF COUNTY LONDONDERRY

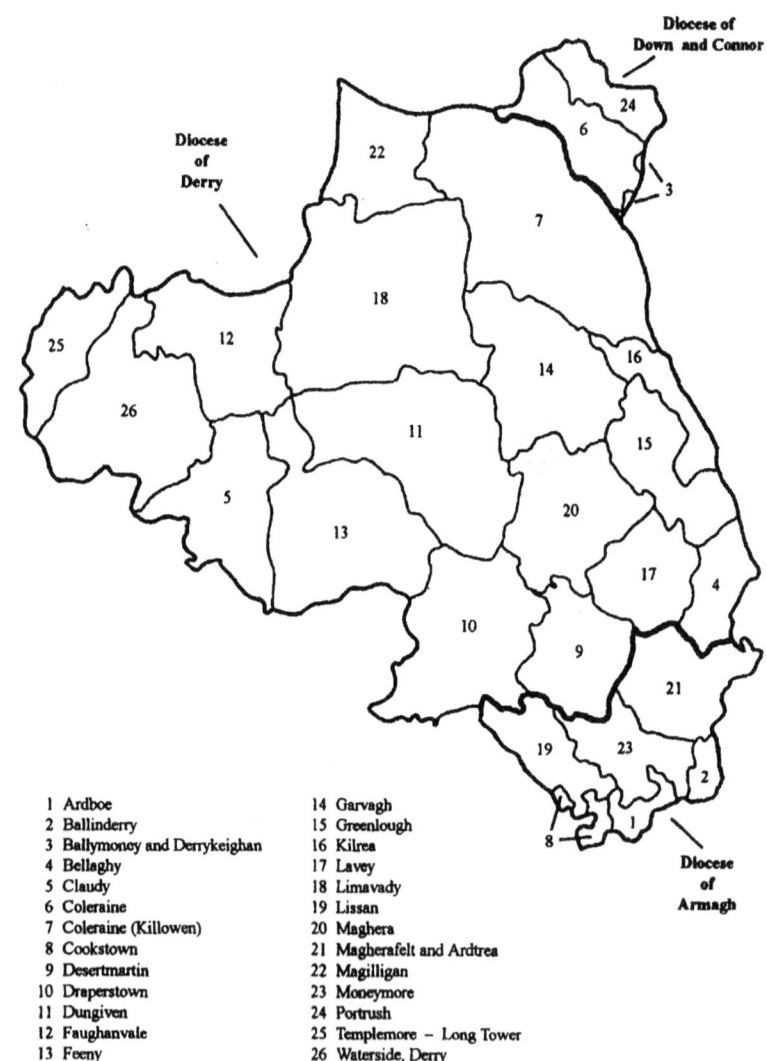

1 Ardboe
2 Ballinderry
3 Ballymoney and Derrykeighan
4 Bellaghy
5 Claudy
6 Coleraine
7 Coleraine (Killowen)
8 Cookstown
9 Desertmartin
10 Draperstown
11 Dungiven
12 Faughanvale
13 Feeny
14 Garvagh
15 Greenlough
16 Kilrea
17 Lavey
18 Limavady
19 Lissan
20 Maghera
21 Magherafelt and Ardtrea
22 Magilligan
23 Moneymore
24 Portrush
25 Templemore – Long Tower
26 Waterside, Derry

THE PRESBYTERIAN CONGREGATIONS
OF COUNTY LONDONDERRY

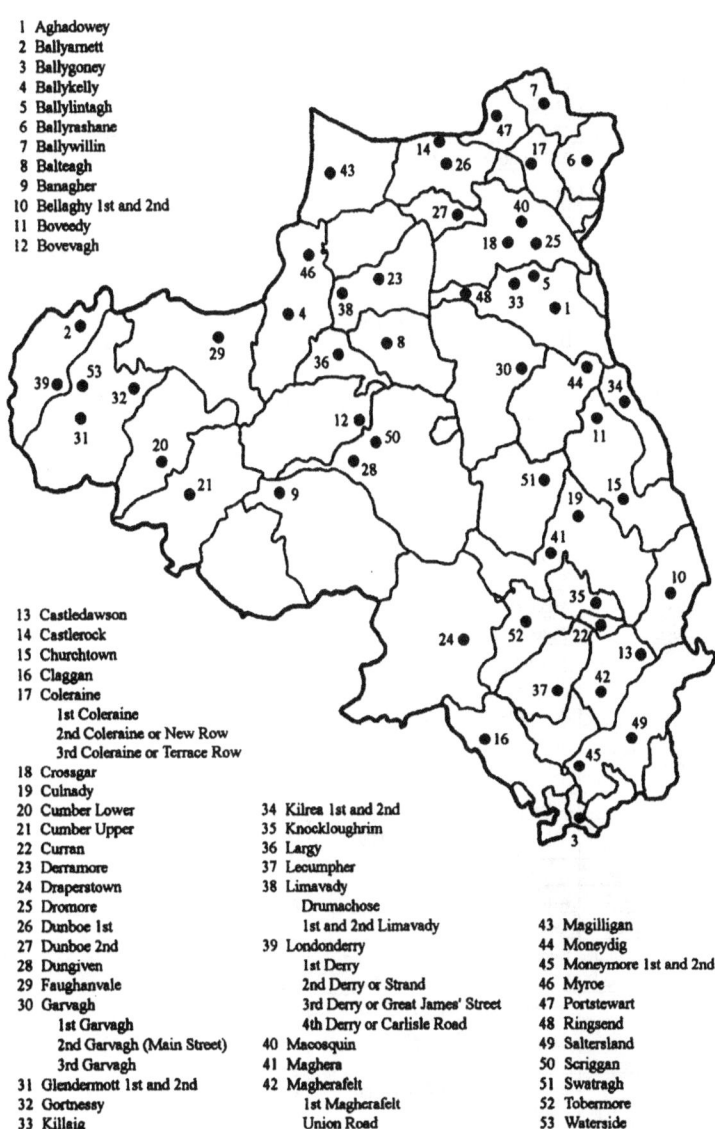

1 Aghadowey
2 Ballyarnett
3 Ballygoney
4 Ballykelly
5 Ballylintagh
6 Ballyrashane
7 Ballywillin
8 Balteagh
9 Banagher
10 Bellaghy 1st and 2nd
11 Boveedy
12 Bovevagh
13 Castledawson
14 Castlerock
15 Churchtown
16 Claggan
17 Coleraine
   1st Coleraine
   2nd Coleraine or New Row
   3rd Coleraine or Terrace Row
18 Crossgar
19 Culnady
20 Cumber Lower
21 Cumber Upper
22 Curran
23 Derramore
24 Draperstown
25 Dromore
26 Dunboe 1st
27 Dunboe 2nd
28 Dungiven
29 Faughanvale
30 Garvagh
   1st Garvagh
   2nd Garvagh (Main Street)
   3rd Garvagh
31 Glendermott 1st and 2nd
32 Gortnessy
33 Killaig
34 Kilrea 1st and 2nd
35 Knockloughrim
36 Largy
37 Lecumpher
38 Limavady
   Drumachose
   1st and 2nd Limavady
39 Londonderry
   1st Derry
   2nd Derry or Strand
   3rd Derry or Great James' Street
   4th Derry or Carlisle Road
40 Macosquin
41 Maghera
42 Magherafelt
   1st Magherafelt
   Union Road
43 Magilligan
44 Moneydig
45 Moneymore 1st and 2nd
46 Myroe
47 Portstewart
48 Ringsend
49 Saltersland
50 Scriggan
51 Swatragh
52 Tobermore
53 Waterside

The Place Names of County Derry

Townland	D.E.D.	Parish	Registrar District	Poor Law Union	17th Century Landowner
Aghadowey	Aghadowey	Aghadowey	Aghadowey	Coleraine	Churchland
Aghagaskin	Magherafelt	Magherafelt	Magherafelt	Magherafelt	Salters
Aghansillagh	Lislane	Balteagh	Limavady	Limavady	Haberdashers
Alla Lower	Claudy	Cumber Upper	Claudy	Londonderry	Churchland
Alla Upper	Claudy	Cumber Upper	Claudy	Londonderry	Churchland
Altaghoney	Ballymullins	Cumber Upper	Claudy	Londonderry	Skinners
Altduff	Glenkeen	Errigal	Garvagh	Coleraine	Ironmongers
Altibrian	Downhill	Formoyle	Articlave	Coleraine	Clothworkers
Altikeeragh	Downhill	Dunboe	Articlave	Coleraine	Clothworkers
Altinure Lower	Banagher	Learmount	Claudy	Londonderry	Skinners
Altinure Upper	Banagher	Learmount	Claudy	Londonderry	Fishmongers
Altnagelvin	Waterside	Clondermot	Waterside Rural	Londonderry	Goldsmiths
Annagh and Moneysterlin	Desertmartin	Desertmartin	Magherafelt	Magherafelt	Churchland
Annaghmore	Castle Dawson	Magherafelt	Bellaghy	Magherafelt	Phillips
Annahavil	Moneyhaw	Arboe	Moneymore	Magherafelt	Drapers
Annahavil	Moneyhaw	Derryloran	Moneymore	Magherafelt	Drapers
Ardagh	Salterstown	Ballinderry	Magherafelt	Magherafelt	Salters
Ardgarvan	Fruithill	Drumachose	Limavady	Limavady	Churchland
Ardground	Bondsglen	Cumber Lower	Claudy	Londonderry	Skinners
Ardina	Articlave	Dunboe	Articlave	Coleraine	Clothworkers
Ardinarive	Straw	Bovevagh	Ballykelly	Limavady	Churchland
Ardkill	Ardmore	Clondermot	Waterside Rural	Londonderry	Grocers
Ardlough	Waterside	Clondermot	Waterside Rural	Londonderry	Churchland
Ardmore	Fruithill	Balteagh	Limavady	Limavady	Churchland
Ardmore	Ardmore	Clondermot	Waterside Rural	Londonderry	Churchland
Ardnabrocky	Waterside	Clondermot	Waterside Rural	Londonderry	Churchland
Ardnaguniog	Lough Enagh	Faughanvale	Eglinton	Londonderry	Grocers
Ardnargle	Myroe	Tamlaght Finlagan	Bellarena	Limavady	Phillips
Ardreagh	Aghadowey	Aghadowey	Aghadowey	Coleraine	Churchland
Ardvarness	Drumcroon	Macosquin	Aghadowey	Coleraine	Merchant Taylors
Articlave Lower	Articlave	Dunboe	Articlave	Coleraine	Clothworkers
Articlave town	Articlave	Dunboe	Articlave	Coleraine	Clothworkers
Articlave Upper	Articlave	Dunboe	Articlave	Coleraine	Clothworkers
Articrunaght North	Knockantern	Ballyrashane	Coleraine	Coleraine	Irish Society
Articrunaght South	Knockantern	Ballyrashane	Coleraine	Coleraine	Irish Society
Artidillon	Articlave	Dunboe	Articlave	Coleraine	Clothworkers
Artikelly	Aghanloo	Aghanloo	Bellarena	Limavady	Haberdashers
Ashlamduff	Glenshane	Dungiven	Dungiven	Limavady	Skinners
Aughil	Benone	Magilligan	Bellarena	Limavady	Churchland
Aughlish	Owenreagh	Banagher	Feeny	Limavady	Churchland

Townland	D.E.D.	Parish	Registrar District	Poor Law Union	17th Century Landowner
Aughrim	Ballyronan	Artrea	Magherafelt	Magherafelt	Salters
Avish	Lough Enagh	Clondermot	Eglinton	Londonderry	Grocers
Avish	Benone	Magilligan	Bellarena	Limavady	Churchland
Back	Myroe	Tamlaght Finlagan	Bellarena	Limavady	Phillips
Ballinderry	Salterstown	Ballinderry	Magherafelt	Magherafelt	Churchland
Ballinderry	Tobermore	Kilcronaghan	Maghera	Magherafelt	Vintners
Ballindreen Irish	Knockantern	Ballyrashane	Coleraine	Coleraine	Irish Society
Ballindreen Scotch	Knockantern	Ballyrashane	Coleraine	Coleraine	Irish Society
Ballindrum	Springhill	Artrea	Moneymore	Magherafelt	Salters
Ballinrees	Aghadowey	Aghadowey	Aghadowey	Coleraine	Churchland
Ballinrees	Letterloan	Formoyle	Articlave	Coleraine	Merchant Taylors
Ballintaggart	Somerset	Macosquin	Aghadowey	Coleraine	Merchant Taylors
Ballinteer North	Bannbrook	Macosquin	Articlave	Coleraine	Clothworkers
Ballinteer South	Bannbrook	Macosquin	Articlave	Coleraine	Clothworkers
Ballintemple	Glenkeen	Errigal	Garvagh	Coleraine	Ironmongers
Balloughry	Liberties Upper	Templemore	Liberties Upper	Londonderry	Irish Society
Ballyagan	Garvagh	Desertoghill	Garvagh	Coleraine	Ironmongers
Ballyarnet	Liberties Lower	Templemore	Liberties Lower	Londonderry	Irish Society
Ballyartan	Ballylagan	Coleraine	Portstewart	Coleraine	Irish Society
Ballyartan	Bondsglen	Cumber Upper	Claudy	Londonderry	Skinners
Ballyavelin North	Fruithill	Drumachose	Limavady	Limavady	Merchant Taylors
Ballyavelin South	Fruithill	Balteagh	Limavady	Limavady	Haberdashers
Ballybriest	Lissan Upper	Lissan	Moneymore	Magherafelt˜	Churchland
Ballybrissell	Aghanloo	Aghanloo	Bellarena	Limavady	Churchland
Ballybritain	Aghadowey	Aghadowey	Aghadowey	Coleraine	Churchland
Ballycaghan	Drumcroon	Aghadowey	Aghadowey	Coleraine	Ironmongers
Ballycairn	Bannbrook	Killowen	Articlave	Coleraine	Clothworkers
Ballycallaghan	Bondsglen	Cumber Upper	Claudy	Londonderry	Skinners
Ballycarton	Aghanloo	Aghanloo	Bellarena	Limavady	Haberdashers
Ballycarton	Bellarena	Magilligan	Bellarena	Limavady	Churchland
Ballycastle	Aghanloo	Aghanloo	Bellarena	Limavady	Haberdashers
Ballyclaber	Knockantern	Coleraine	Coleraine	Coleraine	Irish Society
Ballyclough	Drumcroon	Aghadowey	Aghadowey	Coleraine	Ironmongers
Ballycomlargy	Ballymoghan	Desertlyn	Magherafelt	Magherafelt	Salters
Ballycrum	Keady	Drumachose	Limavady	Limavady	Merchant Taylors
Ballydarrog	The Highlands	Carrick	Ballykelly	Limavady	Phillips
Ballydawley	Springhill	Tamlaght	Moneymore	Magherafelt	Churchland
Ballydawley alias Crosspatrick	Springhill	Artrea	Moneymore	Magherafelt	Churchland
Ballydermot	Bellaghy	Ballyscullion	Bellaghy	Magherafelt	Phillips
Ballydevitt	Aghadowey	Aghadowey	Aghadowey	Coleraine	Churchland

Townland	D.E.D.	Parish	Registrar District	Poor Law Union	17th Century Landowner
Ballydonegan	Feeny	Banagher	Feeny	Limavady	Skinners
Ballydonnell	Salterstown	Ballinderry	Magherafelt	Magherafelt	Salters
Ballydullaghan	The Grove	Desertoghill	KIlrea	Coleraine	Mercers
Ballyeglish	The Loup	Artrea	Moneymore	Magherafelt	Salters
Ballyforlea	Moneyhaw	Derryloran	Moneymore	Magherafelt	Drapers
Ballyforlea	Moneyhaw	Lissan	Moneymore	Magherafelt	Drapers
Ballygallin	Portstewart	Ballyaghran	Portstewart	Coleraine	Irish Society
Ballygan Upper	Knockantern	Ballymoney	Coleraine	Coleraine	Earl of Antrim
Ballygawley	Aghadowey	Aghadowey	Aghadowey	Coleraine	Churchland
Ballygelagh East	Portstewart	Ballyaghran	Portstewart	Coleraine	Irish Society
Ballygelagh West	Portstewart	Ballyaghran	Portstewart	Coleraine	Irish Society
Ballygillen Beg	Salterstown	Artrea	Magherafelt	Magherafelt	Salters
Ballygillen More	Salterstown	Artrea	Magherafelt	Magherafelt	Salters
Ballygonny Beg	Springhill	Arboe	Moneymore	Magherafelt	Drapers
Ballygonny Beg	Springhill	Tamlaght	Moneymore	Magherafelt	Drapers
Ballygonny More	Springhill	Arboe	Moneymore	Magherafelt	Drapers
Ballygonny More	Springhill	Tamlaght	Moneymore	Magherafelt	Drapers
Ballygroll	Tamnaherin	Cumber Lower	Eglinton	Londonderry	Grocers
Ballygruby	Moneymore	Artrea	Moneymore	Magherafelt	Drapers
Ballygudden	Eglinton	Faughanvale	Eglinton	Londonderry	Grocers
Ballyguddin	Dungiven	Dungiven	Dungiven	Limavady	Skinners
Ballygurk	The Loup	Artrea	Moneymore	Magherafelt	Salters
Ballygurk	The Loup	Tamlaght	Moneymore	Magherafelt	Salters
Ballyhacket Glenahorry	Downhill	Dunboe	Articlave	Coleraine	Clothworkers
Ballyhacket Lisawilling	Downhill	Dunboe	Articlave	Coleraine	Clothworkers
Ballyhacket Magilligan	Downhill	Dunboe	Articlave	Coleraine	Clothworkers
Ballyhacket Toberclaw	Downhill	Dunboe	Articlave	Coleraine	Clothworkers
Ballyhanedin	Foreglen	Banagher	Feeny	Limavady	Fishmongers
Ballyhanna	Aghanloo	Aghanloo	Bellarena	Limavady	Haberdashers
Ballyharigan	Drum	Bovevagh	Dungiven	Limavady	Phillips
Ballyheifer	Magherafelt	Magherafelt	Magherafelt	Magherafelt	Salters
Ballyhenry East	Myroe	Aghanloo	Bellarena	Limavady	Phillips
Ballyhenry West	Myroe	Tamlaght Finlagan	Bellarena	Limavady	Phillips
Ballyholly	Foreglen	Cumber Upper	Feeny	Limavady	Fishmongers
Ballykeen	Ballykelly	Tamlaght Finlagan	Ballykelly	Limavady	Fishmongers
Ballykelly	Ballykelly	Tamlaght Finlagan	Ballykelly	Limavady	Fishmongers
Ballykelly Level	Ballykelly	Tamlaght Finlagan	Ballykelly	Limavady	Fishmongers
Ballykelly village	Ballykelly	Tamlaght Finlagan	Ballykelly	Limavady	Fishmongers

Townland	D.E.D.	Parish	Registrar District	Poor Law Union	17th Century Landowner
Ballyknock	Tullykeeran	Killelagh	Maghera	Magherafelt	Vintners
Ballylagan	Somerset	Macosquin	Aghadowey	Coleraine	Merchant Taylors
Ballylagan North	Ballylagan	Ballywillin	Portstewart	Coleraine	Irish Society
Ballylagan South	Ballylagan	Ballywillin	Portstewart	Coleraine	Irish Society
Ballylame	The Grove	Desertoghill	Kilrea	Coleraine	Mercers
Ballyleagry	Fruithill	Balteagh	Limavady	Limavady	Haberdashers
Ballyleese North	Portstewart	Ballyaghran	Portstewart	Coleraine	Irish Society
Ballyleese South	Portstewart	Ballyaghran	Portstewart	Coleraine	Irish Society
Ballyleese West Quarter	Portstewart	Ballyaghran	Portstewart	Coleraine	Irish Society
Ballyleighery Lower	Bellarena	Magilligan	Bellarena	Limavady	Churchland
Ballyleighery Upper	Bellarena	Magilligan	Bellarena	Limavady	Churchland
Ballylifford	Salterstown	Ballinderry	Magherafelt	Magherafelt	Salters
Ballylintagh	Drumcroon	Aghadowey	Aghadowey	Coleraine	Ironmongers
Ballylintagh	Drumcroon	Macosquin	Aghadowey	Coleraine	Ironmongers
Ballyloughan	Moneyhaw	Derryloran	Moneymore	Magherafelt	Drapers
Ballymacallion	Gelvin	Dungiven	Dungiven	Limavady	Haberdashers
Ballymacilcurr	Maghera	Maghera	Maghera	Magherafelt	Vintners
Ballymaclanigan	Foreglen	Cumber Upper	Feeny	Limavady	Fishmongers
Ballymaclary	Benone	Magilligan	Bellarena	Limavady	Churchland
Ballymaclevennon East	Ballylagan	Ballywillin	Portstewart	Coleraine	Irish Society
Ballymaclevennon West	Ballylagan	Ballywillin	Portstewart	Coleraine	Irish Society
Ballymacombs Beg	Bellaghy	Ballyscullion	Bellaghy	Magherafelt	Vintners
Ballymacombs More	Bellaghy	Ballyscullion	Bellaghy	Magherafelt	Vintners
Ballymacpeake Lower	Clady	Tamlaght O'Crilly	Bellaghy	Magherafelt	Churchland
Ballymacpeake Upper	Rocktown	Maghera	Bellaghy	Magherafelt	Vintners
Ballymacpherson	Desertmartin	Desertmartin	Magherafelt	Magherafelt	Churchland
Ballymacran	Myroe	Tamlaght Finlagan	Bellarena	Limavady	Phillips
Ballymadigan	Downhill	Dunboe	Articlave	Coleraine	Churchland
Ballymaglin	Aghanloo	Aghanloo	Bellarena	Limavady	Haberdashers
Ballymagoland	Benone	Magilligan	Bellarena	Limavady	Churchland
Ballymagowan	Londonderry Urban No. 2	Templemore	Londonderry Urban No. 2	Londonderry	Irish Society
Ballymagowan	Liberties Upper	Templemore	Liberties Upper	Londonderry	Irish Society
Ballymagrorty	Liberties Lower	Templemore	Liberties Lower	Londonderry	Irish Society
Ballymaguigan	Castle Dawson	Artrea	Bellaghy	Magherafelt	Phillips
Ballymakeever	Dungiven	Dungiven	Dungiven	Limavady	Skinners
Ballymenagh	Ringsend	Aghadowey	Aghadowey	Coleraine	Merchant Taylors

Townland	D.E.D.	Parish	Registrar District	Poor Law Union	17th Century Landowner
Ballymenagh	The Grove	Desertoghill	Kilrea	Coleraine	Mercers
Ballymoghan Beg	Ballymoghan	Magherafelt	Magherafelt	Magherafelt	Salters
Ballymoghan More	Ballymoghan	Magherafelt	Magherafelt	Magherafelt	Salters
Ballymonan	Dungiven	Dungiven	Dungiven	Limavady	Skinners
Ballymoney	Drum	Bovevagh	Dungiven	Limavady	Phillips
Ballymoney	Articlave	Dunboe	Articlave	Coleraine	Clothworkers
Ballymoney	Aghanloo	Aghanloo	Bellarena	Limavady	Haberdashers
Ballymore	The Highlands	Carrick	Ballykelly	Limavady	Phillips
Ballymoyle	Springhill	Tamlaght	Moneymore	Magherafelt	Drapers
Ballymuckleheany	Ballymoghan	Desertlyn	Magherafelt	Magherafelt	Salters
Ballymulderg Beg	Ballyronan	Artrea	Magherafelt	Magherafelt	Salters
Ballymulderg More	Ballyronan	Artrea	Magherafelt	Magherafelt	Salters
Ballymulholland	Bellarena	Magilligan	Bellarena	Limavady	Churchland
Ballymulligan	The Loup	Artrea	Moneymore	Magherafelt	Salters
Ballymully	Fruithill	Balteagh	Limavady	Limavady	Churchland
Ballymully	Moneymore	Desertlyn	Moneymore	Magherafelt	Churchland
Ballymultimber	Bellarena	Magilligan	Bellarena	Limavady	Churchland
Ballymultrea	Salterstown	Ballinderry	Magherafelt	Magherafelt	Salters
Ballynacally Beg	Aghadowey	Aghadowey	Aghadowey	Coleraine	Churchland
Ballynacally More	Aghadowey	Aghadowey	Aghadowey	Coleraine	Churchland
Ballynacanon	Letterloan	Macosquin	Articlave	Coleraine	Merchant Taylors
Ballynacross	Gulladuff	Maghera	Maghera	Magherafelt	Vintners
Ballynag Lower	Knockantern	Ballyrashane	Coleraine	Coleraine	Irish Society
Ballynag Upper	Knockantern	Ballyrashane	Coleraine	Coleraine	Irish Society
Ballynagagalliagh	Liberties Lower	Templemore	Liberties Lower	Londonderry	Churchland
Ballynagard	Liberties Lower	Templemore	Liberties Lower	Londonderry	Churchland
Ballynagarve	Ballyronan	Artrea	Magherafelt	Magherafelt	Salters
Ballynagown	Desertmartin	Desertmartin	Magherafelt	Magherafelt	Churchland
Ballynahery	Fruithill	Drumachose	Limavady	Limavady	Merchant Taylors
Ballynahone Beg	Maghera	Maghera	Maghera	Magherafelt	Churchland
Ballynahone More	Tobermore	Termoneeny	Maghera	Magherafelt	Churchland
Ballynameen	Garvagh	Desertoghill	Garvagh	Coleraine	Churchland
Ballynamore	Tamnaherin	Cumber Lower	Eglinton	Londonderry	Goldsmiths
Ballynashallog	Liberties Lower	Templemore	Liberties Lower	Londonderry	Irish Society
Ballynease-Helton	Bellaghy	Ballyscullion	Bellaghy	Magherafelt	Vintners
Ballynease-Macpeake	Bellaghy	Ballyscullion	Bellaghy	Magherafelt	Vintners
Ballynease-Strain	Bellaghy	Ballyscullion	Bellaghy	Magherafelt	Vintners
Ballyneill Beg	The Loup	Artrea	Moneymore	Magherafelt	Salters
Ballyneill More	The Loup	Artrea	Moneymore	Magherafelt	Salters
Ballynenagh	The Loup	Artrea	Moneymore	Magherafelt	Salters

Townland	D.E.D.	Parish	Registrar District	Poor Law Union	17th Century Landowner
Ballyness	Gelvin	Dungiven	Dungiven	Limavady	Haberdashers
Ballyness	Somerset	Macosquin	Aghadowey	Coleraine	Churchland
Ballynewy	Springhill	Artrea	Moneymore	Magherafelt	Churchland
Ballynian	The Grove	Tamlaght O'Crilly	Kilrea	Coleraine	Mercers
Ballynocker	Magherafelt	Magherafelt	Magherafelt	Magherafelt	Salters
Ballynure	Carnamoney	Ballynascreen	Draperstown	Magherafelt	Drapers
Ballyoan	Lough Enagh	Clondermot	Eglinton	Londonderry	Churchland
Ballyore	Glendermot	Clondermot	Waterside Rural	Londonderry	Goldsmiths
Ballyquin	Fruithill	Carrick	Limavady	Limavady	Phillips
Ballyreagh	Ballylagan	Ballywillin	Portstewart	Coleraine	Irish Society
Ballyriff	The Loup	Artrea	Moneymore	Magherafelt	Salters
Ballyrisk Beg	Keady	Drumachose	Limavady	Limavady	Haberdashers
Ballyrisk More	Keady	Drumachose	Limavady	Limavady	Haberdashers
Ballyrogan	Glenkeen	Errigal	Garvagh	Coleraine	Ironmongers
Ballyrogully	The Loup	Artrea	Moneymore	Magherafelt	Salters
Ballyronan Beg	Salterstown	Ballinderry	Magherafelt	Magherafelt	Salters
Ballyronan More	Ballyronan	Artrea	Magherafelt	Magherafelt	Salters
Ballyrory	Ballymullins	Learmount	Claudy	Londonderry	Fishmongers
Ballysally	Portstewart	Ballyaghran	Portstewart	Coleraine	Irish Society
Ballysally	Portstewart	Coleraine	Portstewart	Coleraine	Irish Society
Ballyscullion	Bellarena	Magilligan	Bellarena	Limavady	Churchland
Ballyscullion West	Bellaghy	Ballyscullion	Bellaghy	Magherafelt	Churchland
Ballyshasky	Ardmore	Clondermot	Waterside Rural	Londonderry	Grocers
Ballyspallan	Ballykelly	Tamlaght Finlagan	Ballykelly	Limavady	Fishmongers
Ballystrone	Articlave	Formoyle	Articlave	Coleraine	Clothworkers
Ballyvelton Lower	Knockantern	Ballyrashane	Coleraine	Coleraine	Irish Society
Ballyvelton Upper	Knockantern	Ballyrashane	Coleraine	Coleraine	Irish Society
Ballyvennox	Drumcroon	Macosquin	Aghadowey	Coleraine	Merchant Taylors
Ballyversall	Knockantern	Ballyrashane	Coleraine	Coleraine	Irish Society
Ballywildrick Lower	Articlave	Dunboe	Articlave	Coleraine	Clothworkers
Ballywildrick Upper	Articlave	Dunboe	Articlave	Coleraine	Clothworkers
Ballywilliam	Drumcroon	Macosquin	Aghadowey	Coleraine	Ironmongers
Ballywillin	Aghadowey	Aghadowey	Aghadowey	Coleraine	Churchland
Ballywillin Bog	Ballylagan	Ballywillin	Portstewart	Coleraine	Irish Society
Ballywindelland Lower	Knockantern	Ballymoney	Coleraine	Coleraine	Earl of Antrim
Ballywindelland Upper	Knockantern	Ballymoney	Coleraine	Coleraine	Earl of Antrim
Ballywoodock	Downhill	Dunboe	Articlave	Coleraine	Churchland
Ballywoolen	Articlave	Dunboe	Articlave	Coleraine	Clothworkers
Balteagh Lower	Letterloan	Macosquin	Articlave	Coleraine	Merchant Taylors

Townland	D.E.D.	Parish	Registrar District	Poor Law Union	17th Century Landowner
Balteagh Upper	Letterloan	Macosquin	Articlave	Coleraine	Merchant Taylors
Bancran Glebe	Bancran	Ballynascreen	Draperstown	Magherafelt	Churchland
Bannbrook Lower	Bannbrook	Dunboe	Articlave	Coleraine	Churchland
Bannbrook Upper	Bannbrook	Dunboe	Articlave	Coleraine	Churchland
Barnakilly	Faughanvale	Faughanvale	Ballykelly	Limavady	Fishmongers
Barr Cregg	Claudy	Cumber Upper	Claudy	Londonderry	Churchland
Beagh (Spiritual)	Maghera	Maghera	Maghera	Magherafelt	Churchland
Beagh (Temporal)	Swatragh	Killelagh	Maghera	Magherafelt	Mercers
Belagherty	Salterstown	Ballinderry	Magherafelt	Magherafelt	Salters
Belgarrow	Articlave	Formoyle	Articlave	Coleraine	Clothworkers
Bellaghy town	Bellaghy	Ballyscullion	Bellaghy	Magherafelt	Vintners
Bellany	Bannbrook	Dunboe	Articlave	Coleraine	Churchland
Bellarena	Bellarena	Magilligan	Bellarena	Limavady	Churchland
Bellasses	Knockantern	Coleraine	Coleraine	Coleraine	Irish Society
Bellemont More	Portstewart	Ballyaghran	Portstewart	Coleraine	Irish Society
Bellemont North	Portstewart	Ballyaghran	Portstewart	Coleraine	Irish Society
Bellemont South	Portstewart	Ballyaghran	Portstewart	Coleraine	Irish Society
Bellury	Garvagh	Desertoghill	Garvagh	Coleraine	Ironmongers
Belraugh	Ringsend	Errigal	Aghadowey	Coleraine	Ironmongers
Bennarees	Downhill	Dunboe	Articlave	Coleraine	Churchland
Benone	Benone	Magilligan	Bellarena	Limavady	Churchland
Big Glebe	Downhill	Dunboe	Articlave	Coleraine	Churchland
Binn	Claudy	Cumber Upper	Claudy	Londonderry	Churchland
Blagh	Ballylagan	Coleraine	Portstewart	Coleraine	Irish Society
Blakes Lower	Bannbrook	Dunboe	Articlave	Coleraine	Churchland
Blakes Upper	Bannbrook	Dunboe	Articlave	Coleraine	Churchland
Bogagh	Glendermot	Clondermot	Waterside Rural	Londonderry	Goldsmiths
Boghilboy	Bovagh	Desertoghill	Garvagh	Coleraine	Ironmongers
Boghill	Ballylagan	Coleraine	Portstewart	Coleraine	Irish Society
Bogtown	Articlave	Dunboe	Articlave	Coleraine	Clothworkers
Bogtown (part of)	Articlave	Dunboe	Articlave	Coleraine	Clothworkers
Bolea	Keady	Drumachose	Limavady	Limavady	Haberdashers
Boleran	Glenkeen	Errigal	Garvagh	Coleraine	Ironmongers
Bolie	Faughanvale	Faughanvale	Ballykelly	Limavady	Churchland
Bolies	Glendermot	Clondermot	Waterside Rural	Londonderry	Goldsmiths
Bonnanaboigh	Straw	Bovevagh	Ballykelly	Limavady	Phillips
Bovagh	Bovagh	Aghadowey	Garvagh	Coleraine	Ironmongers
Bovally	Fruithill	Drumachose	Limavady	Limavady	Churchland
Boveagh	Iniscarn	Desertmartin	Draperstown	Magherafelt	Drapers
Bovedy	Hervey Hill	Tamlaght O'Crilly	Kilrea	Coleraine	Mercers
Bovevagh	Straw	Bovevagh	Ballykelly	Limavady	Churchland
Boviel	Glenshane	Dungiven	Dungiven	Limavady	Skinners

Townland	D.E.D.	Parish	Registrar District	Poor Law Union	17th Century Landowner
Bracaghreilly	Carnamoney	Maghera	Draperstown	Magherafelt	Drapers
Brackagh	Bancran	Ballynascreen	Draperstown	Magherafelt	Skinners
Brackagh	Lissan Upper	Lissan	Moneymore	Magherafelt	Churchland
Brackagh Slieve Gallion	Brackagh Slieve Gallion	Desertmartin	Moneymore	Magherafelt	Drapers
Brackaghlislea	Iniscarn	Kilcronaghan	Draperstown	Magherafelt	Drapers
Brackfield	Bondsglen	Cumber Lower	Claudy	Londonderry	Skinners
Bratwell	Downhill	Formoyle	Articlave	Coleraine	Clothworkers
Brickkilns	Glendermot	Clondermot	Waterside Rural	Londonderry	Goldsmiths
Brishey	Dungiven	Dungiven	Dungiven	Limavady	Skinners
Broagh	Rocktown	Termoneeny	Bellaghy	Magherafelt	Vintners
Brockagh	Tamnaherin	Cumber Lower	Eglinton	Londonderry	Grocers
Brockagh	Glenkeen	Errigal	Garvagh	Coleraine	Ironmongers
Brockaghboy	Slaght	Errigal	Garvagh	Coleraine	Ironmongers
Broglasco	Myroe	Tamlaght Finlagan	Bellarena	Limavady	Fishmongers
Broharris	Ballykelly	Tamlaght Finlagan	Ballykelly	Limavady	Fishmongers
Broighter	Myroe	Tamlaght Finlagan	Bellarena	Limavady	Fishmongers
Burnally	Myroe	Tamlaght Finlagan	Bellarena	Limavady	Phillips
Burren Beg	Downhill	Dunboe	Articlave	Coleraine	Churchland
Burren More	Downhill	Dunboe	Articlave	Coleraine	Churchland
Bushtown	Somerset	Macosquin	Aghadowey	Coleraine	Merchant Taylors
Cabragh	Rocktown	Termoneeny	Bellaghy	Magherafelt	Vintners
Cah	Garvagh	Errigal	Garvagh	Coleraine	Ironmongers
Caheny	Bovagh	Aghadowey	Garvagh	Coleraine	Ironmongers
Cahery	Fruithill	Drumachose	Limavady	Limavady	Churchland
Cahore	Draperstown	Ballynascreen	Draperstown	Magherafelt	Skinners
Calmore	Tobermore	Kilcronaghan	Maghera	Magherafelt	Drapers
Cam	Letterloan	Macosquin	Articlave	Coleraine	Merchant Taylors
Camnish	Gelvin	Bovevagh	Dungiven	Limavady	Haberdashers
Campsie Lower	Eglinton	Faughanvale	Eglinton	Londonderry	Grocers
Campsie Upper	Eglinton	Faughanvale	Eglinton	Londonderry	Grocers
Camus	Somerset	Macosquin	Aghadowey	Coleraine	Churchland
Camus Macosquin Glebe	Drumcroon	Macosquin	Aghadowey	Coleraine	Churchland
Caneese	Lissan Upper	Lissan	Moneymore	Magherafelt	Churchland
Cappagh Beg	Portstewart	Ballyaghran	Portstewart	Coleraine	Irish Society
Cappagh More	Portstewart	Ballyaghran	Portstewart	Coleraine	Irish Society
Carbalintober	The Grove	Desertoghill	Kilrea	Coleraine	Mercers
Carbullion	Aghanloo	Aghanloo	Bellarena	Limavady	Haberdashers
Carlaragh	The Highlands	Tamlaght Finlagan	Ballykelly	Limavady	Phillips

Townland	D.E.D.	Parish	Registrar District	Poor Law Union	17th Century Landowner
Carmean	Brackagh Slieve Gallion	Desertlyn	Moneymore	Magherafelt	Drapers
Carmoney	Eglinton	Faughanvale	Eglinton	Londonderry	Grocers
Carn	Lough Enagh	Clondermot	Eglinton	Londonderry	Churchland
Carn	Glenshane	Dungiven	Dungiven	Limavady	Skinners
Carnaboy	Ballylagan	Ballywillin	Portstewart	Coleraine	Irish Society
Carnafarn	Glendermot	Clondermot	Waterside Rural	Londonderry	Goldsmiths
Carnakilly Lower	Eglinton	Faughanvale	Eglinton	Londonderry	Grocers
Carnakilly Upper	Eglinton	Faughanvale	Eglinton	Londonderry	Grocers
Carnalbanagh	Portstewart	Ballyaghran	Portstewart	Coleraine	Irish Society
Carnalridge	Ballylagan	Ballywillin	Portstewart	Coleraine	Irish Society
Carnamoney	Carnamoney	Ballynascreen	Draperstown	Magherafelt	Drapers
Carnamuff	Faughanvale	Faughanvale	Ballykelly	Limavady	Fishmongers
Carnanbane	Owenreagh	Banagher	Feeny	Limavady	Churchland
Carnanbane	Ballymullins	Learmount	Claudy	Londonderry	Fishmongers
Carnanee	Portstewart	Ballyaghran	Portstewart	Coleraine	Irish Society
Carnanreagh	Ballymullins	Learmount	Claudy	Londonderry	Fishmongers
Carncose	Brackagh Slieve Gallion	Desertmartin	Moneymore	Magherafelt	Drapers
Carndaisy	Brackagh Slieve Gallion	Desertlyn	Moneymore	Magherafelt	Drapers
Carndougan	Somerset	Macosquin	Aghadowey	Coleraine	Merchant Taylors
Carneety	Articlave	Dunboe	Articlave	Coleraine	Clothworkers
Carnet	Fruithill	Balteagh	Limavady	Limavady	Haberdashers
Carnowry	Benone	Magilligan	Bellarena	Limavady	Churchland
Carrakeel	Lough Enagh	Clondermot	Eglinton	Londonderry	Grocers
Carraloan	Ballyronan	Artrea	Magherafelt	Magherafelt	Churchland
Carran	Fruithill	Drumachose	Limavady	Limavady	Churchland
Carranrallagh	Aghadowey	Aghadowey	Aghadowey	Coleraine	Churchland
Carranroe	Kilrea	Aghadowey	Kilrea	Coleraine	Mercers
Carrick	Straw	Carrick	Ballykelly	Limavady	Phillips
Carrick East	Fruithill	Carrick	Limavady	Limavady	Phillips
Carrickhugh	Faughanvale	Faughanvale	Ballykelly	Limavady	Fishmongers
Carricknakielt	Maghera	Termoneeny	Maghera	Magherafelt	Churchland
Carrowclare	Myroe	Tamlaght Finlagan	Bellarena	Limavady	Phillips
Carrowmenagh	Tullykeeran	Killelagh	Maghera	Magherafelt	Churchland
Carrowmenagh	Myroe	Tamlaght Finlagan	Bellarena	Limavady	Phillips
Carrowmuddle	Myroe	Tamlaght Finlagan	Bellarena	Limavady	Phillips
Carrowreagh	Garvagh	Desertoghill	Garvagh	Coleraine	Ironmongers
Carrowreagh	Bellarena	Magilligan	Bellarena	Limavady	Churchland
Carrowreagh	Myroe	Tamlaght Finlagan	Bellarena	Limavady	Phillips
Carrydarragh	Moneymore	Desertlyn	Moneymore	Magherafelt	Churchland

Townland	D.E.D.	Parish	Registrar District	Poor Law Union	17th Century Landowner
Carrydoo	Keady	Drumachose	Limavady	Limavady	Haberdashers
Cashel	Glenshane	Dungiven	Dungiven	Limavady	Skinners
Cashel	Letterloan	Macosquin	Articlave	Coleraine	Merchant Taylors
Castle Dawson town	Castle Dawson	Magherafelt	Bellaghy	Magherafelt	Phillips
Castlerock town, Freehall Dunlop	Downhill	Dunboe	Articlave	Coleraine	Clothworkers
Castlerock town, Freehall Watson	Downhill	Dunboe	Articlave	Coleraine	Clothworkers
Castleroe	Somerset	Macosquin	Aghadowey	Coleraine	Churchland
Castletoodry	Bannbrook	Killowen	Articlave	Coleraine	Clothworkers
Caulhame	Bovagh	Desertoghill	Garvagh	Coleraine	Ironmongers
Cavanreagh	The Six Towns	Ballynascreen	Draperstown	Magherafelt	Churchland
Caw	Waterside	Clondermot	Waterside Rural	Londonderry	Churchland
Church Island	Bellaghy	Ballyscullion	Bellaghy	Magherafelt	Churchland
Churchland	Bannbrook	Killowen	Articlave	Coleraine	Churchland
Clagan	Agivey	Aghadowey	Aghadowey	Coleraine	Ironmongers
Clagan	Banagher	Learmount	Claudy	Londonderry	Fishmongers
Clagan	Lissan Upper	Lissan	Moneymore	Magherafelt	Churchland
Clagan	Bellarena	Magilligan	Bellarena	Limavady	Churchland
Clagan	The Highlands	Tamlaght Finlagan	Ballykelly	Limavady	Phillips
Clampernow	Glendermot	Clondermot	Waterside Rural	Londonderry	Goldsmiths
Clanterkee	Eglinton	Faughanvale	Eglinton	Londonderry	Grocers
Claragh	Kilrea	Kilrea	Kilrea	Coleraine	Mercers
Clarehill	Agivey	Aghadowey	Aghadowey	Coleraine	Ironmongers
Claudy	Claudy	Cumber Upper	Claudy	Londonderry	Churchland
Claudy town	Claudy	Cumber Upper	Claudy	Londonderry	Churchland
Clintagh	Drumcroon	Aghadowey	Aghadowey	Coleraine	Ironmongers
Cloane	Carnamoney	Ballynascreen	Draperstown	Magherafelt	Drapers
Cloghan	Lislane	Balteagh	Limavady	Limavady	Haberdashers
Cloghog	Moneyhaw	Derryloran	Moneymore	Magherafelt	Drapers
Cloghole	Lough Enagh	Faughanvale	Eglinton	Londonderry	Grocers
Cloghore or Greerstown	Glendermot	Clondermot	Waterside Rural	Londonderry	Goldsmiths
Clondermot	Ardmore	Clondermot	Waterside Rural	Londonderry	Churchland
Clonmakane	Tamnaherin	Cumber Lower	Eglinton	Londonderry	Grocers
Clooney	Aghanloo	Aghanloo	Bellarena	Limavady	Haberdashers
Clooney	Waterside	Clondermot	Waterside Urban	Londonderry	Churchland
Clooney	Tobermore	Kilcronaghan	Maghera	Magherafelt	Drapers
Clooney	Benone	Magilligan	Bellarena	Limavady	Churchland
Cloughfin	Bancran	Ballynascreen	Draperstown	Magherafelt	Skinners
Cloughfin	Iniscarn	Kilcronaghan	Draperstown	Magherafelt	Drapers
Cloughglass	Londonderry Urban No. 1	Templemore	Londonderry Urban No. 2	Londonderry	Irish Society

Townland	D.E.D.	Parish	Registrar District	Poor Law Union	17th Century Landowner
Cloyfin North	Ballylagan	Ballywillin	Portstewart	Coleraine	Irish Society
Cloyfin South	Knockantern	Ballyrashane	Coleraine	Coleraine	Irish Society
Cluntygeeragh	Glenshane	Dungiven	Dungiven	Limavady	Skinners
Colebreene Lower	Knockantern	Ballymoney	Coleraine	Coleraine	Earl of Antrim
Coleraine, Abbey Street	Coleraine	Coleraine	Coleraine	Coleraine	Irish Society
Coleraine, Adams Row	Coleraine	Coleraine	Coleraine	Coleraine	Irish Society
Coleraine, Adelaide Avenue	Coleraine	Coleraine	Coleraine	Coleraine	Irish Society
Coleraine, Albert Terrace	Coleraine	Coleraine	Coleraine	Coleraine	Irish Society
Coleraine, Alexander Terrace	Coleraine	Coleraine	Coleraine	Coleraine	Irish Society
Coleraine, Alma Place	Coleraine	Coleraine	Coleraine	Coleraine	Irish Society
Coleraine, Alma Row	Coleraine	Coleraine	Coleraine	Coleraine	Irish Society
Coleraine, Ardbana Terrace	Coleraine	Coleraine	Coleraine	Coleraine	Irish Society
Coleraine, Arthur Place	Coleraine	Coleraine	Coleraine	Coleraine	Irish Society
Coleraine, Ashley Villa	Coleraine	Killowen	Coleraine	Coleraine	Churchland
Coleraine, Ballycastle Road	Coleraine	Coleraine	Coleraine	Coleraine	Irish Society
Coleraine, Ballycastle Road	Coleraine	Coleraine	Coleraine	Coleraine	Irish Society
Coleraine, Ballymoney Road	Coleraine	Coleraine	Coleraine	Coleraine	Irish Society
Coleraine, Bannfield Road	Coleraine	Coleraine	Coleraine	Coleraine	Irish Society
Coleraine, Baptist Lane	Coleraine	Coleraine	Coleraine	Coleraine	Irish Society
Coleraine, Bellhouse Lane	Coleraine	Coleraine	Coleraine	Coleraine	Irish Society
Coleraine, Bellview Terrace	Coleraine	Coleraine	Coleraine	Coleraine	Irish Society
Coleraine, Beresford Place	Coleraine	Coleraine	Coleraine	Coleraine	Irish Society
Coleraine, Blindgate Street	Coleraine	Coleraine	Coleraine	Coleraine	Irish Society
Coleraine, Boilingwell Lane	Coleraine	Coleraine	Coleraine	Coleraine	Irish Society
Coleraine, Boyds Row	Coleraine	Coleraine	Coleraine	Coleraine	Irish Society
Coleraine, Bridge Street	Coleraine	Coleraine	Coleraine	Coleraine	Irish Society
Coleraine, Brook Street	Coleraine	Coleraine	Coleraine	Coleraine	Irish Society
Coleraine, Brook Street North	Coleraine	Coleraine	Coleraine	Coleraine	Irish Society
Coleraine, Bruces Terrace	Coleraine	Killowen	Coleraine	Coleraine	Churchland
Coleraine, Bushmills Road	Coleraine	Coleraine	Coleraine	Coleraine	Irish Society

Townland	D.E.D.	Parish	Registrar District	Poor Law Union	17th Century Landowner
Coleraine, Captain Street Lower	Coleraine	Killowen	Coleraine	Coleraine	Churchland
Coleraine, Captain Street Upper	Coleraine	Killowen	Coleraine	Coleraine	Churchland
Coleraine, Castleview Road	Coleraine	Coleraine	Coleraine	Coleraine	Irish Society
Coleraine, Chapel Square	Coleraine	Coleraine	Coleraine	Coleraine	Irish Society
Coleraine, Church Street	Coleraine	Coleraine	Coleraine	Coleraine	Irish Society
Coleraine, Churches Walls	Coleraine	Coleraine	Coleraine	Coleraine	Irish Society
Coleraine, Churchland	Coleraine	Killowen	Coleraine	Coleraine	Churchland
Coleraine, Circular Road	Coleraine	Coleraine	Coleraine	Coleraine	Irish Society
Coleraine, Clifton Terrace	Coleraine	Coleraine	Coleraine	Coleraine	Irish Society
Coleraine, Court to rear of Shuttle Hill	Coleraine	Killowen	Coleraine	Coleraine	Churchland
Coleraine, Cross Lane	Coleraine	Coleraine	Coleraine	Coleraine	Irish Society
Coleraine, Dunedin Terrace	Coleraine	Coleraine	Coleraine	Coleraine	Irish Society
Coleraine, Dunlop Street	Coleraine	Killowen	Coleraine	Coleraine	Churchland
Coleraine, Esdale Terrace	Coleraine	Coleraine	Coleraine	Coleraine	Irish Society
Coleraine, Ferryquay Street	Coleraine	Coleraine	Coleraine	Coleraine	Irish Society
Coleraine, Fountainview Terrace	Coleraine	Coleraine	Coleraine	Coleraine	Irish Society
Coleraine, Hamilton Terrace	Coleraine	Killowen	Coleraine	Coleraine	Churchland
Coleraine, Hanover Gardens	Coleraine	Coleraine	Coleraine	Coleraine	Irish Society
Coleraine, Hanover Place	Coleraine	Coleraine	Coleraine	Coleraine	Irish Society
Coleraine, Harpurs Hill	Coleraine	Coleraine	Coleraine	Coleraine	Irish Society
Coleraine, Hartford Place	Coleraine	Coleraine	Coleraine	Coleraine	Irish Society
Coleraine, Hawthorn Terrace	Coleraine	Coleraine	Coleraine	Coleraine	Irish Society
Coleraine, Institution Road	Coleraine	Killowen	Coleraine	Coleraine	Churchland
Coleraine, James Street	Coleraine	Coleraine	Coleraine	Coleraine	Irish Society
Coleraine, Jubilee Terrace	Coleraine	Coleraine	Coleraine	Coleraine	Irish Society
Coleraine, Killowen Street	Coleraine	Killowen	Coleraine	Coleraine	Churchland
Coleraine, Kings Gate Street	Coleraine	Coleraine	Coleraine	Coleraine	Irish Society
Coleraine, Kyles Brae	Coleraine	Killowen	Coleraine	Coleraine	Churchland

Townland	D.E.D.	Parish	Registrar District	Poor Law Union	17th Century Landowner
Coleraine, Landscape Terrace	Coleraine	Killowen	Coleraine	Coleraine	Churchland
Coleraine, Lane off Captain Street Lower	Coleraine	Killowen	Coleraine	Coleraine	Churchland
Coleraine, Laurel Hill	Coleraine	Killowen	Coleraine	Coleraine	Churchland
Coleraine, Lime Market Street	Coleraine	Coleraine	Coleraine	Coleraine	Irish Society
Coleraine, Lodge Road	Coleraine	Coleraine	Coleraine	Coleraine	Irish Society
Coleraine, Long Commons Street	Coleraine	Coleraine	Coleraine	Coleraine	Irish Society
Coleraine, Margaretta Terrace	Coleraine	Coleraine	Coleraine	Coleraine	Irish Society
Coleraine, Masonic Place	Coleraine	Coleraine	Coleraine	Coleraine	Irish Society
Coleraine, Mill Street	Coleraine	Coleraine	Coleraine	Coleraine	Irish Society
Coleraine, Mill Street	Coleraine	Coleraine	Coleraine	Coleraine	Irish Society
Millbank Cottage					
Coleraine, Millbank Terrace	Coleraine	Coleraine	Coleraine	Coleraine	Irish Society
Coleraine, Millburn	Coleraine	Coleraine	Coleraine	Coleraine	Irish Society
Coleraine, Millburn Cottages	Coleraine	Coleraine	Coleraine	Coleraine	Irish Society
Coleraine, Mountsandel Road	Coleraine	Coleraine	Coleraine	Coleraine	Irish Society
Coleraine, Mountsandel Road	Coleraine	Coleraine	Coleraine	Coleraine	Irish Society
Coleraine, New Market Street	Coleraine	Coleraine	Coleraine	Coleraine	Irish Society
Coleraine, New Road Patrick Street	Coleraine	Coleraine	Coleraine	Coleraine	Irish Society
Coleraine, New Row Street	Coleraine	Coleraine	Coleraine	Coleraine	Irish Society
Coleraine, New Row Upper	Coleraine	Coleraine	Coleraine	Coleraine	Irish Society
Coleraine, New Row West	Coleraine	Coleraine	Coleraine	Coleraine	Irish Society
Coleraine, North Rampart	Coleraine	Coleraine	Coleraine	Coleraine	Irish Society
Coleraine, Nursery Road	Coleraine	Coleraine	Coleraine	Coleraine	Irish Society
Coleraine, Olphert Place	Coleraine	Coleraine	Coleraine	Coleraine	Irish Society
Coleraine, Pates Lane	Coleraine	Killowen	Coleraine	Coleraine	Churchland
Coleraine, Portrush Road	Coleraine	Coleraine	Coleraine	Coleraine	Irish Society
Coleraine, Portstewart Road	Coleraine	Coleraine	Coleraine	Coleraine	Irish Society
Coleraine, Queens Street	Coleraine	Coleraine	Coleraine	Coleraine	Irish Society

Townland	D.E.D.	Parish	Registrar District	Poor Law Union	17th Century Landowner
Coleraine, Railway Road	Coleraine	Coleraine	Coleraine	Coleraine	Irish Society
Coleraine, Railway Street	Coleraine	Coleraine	Coleraine	Coleraine	Irish Society
Coleraine, Reids Terrace	Coleraine	Coleraine	Coleraine	Coleraine	Irish Society
Coleraine, Rosmary Lane	Coleraine	Coleraine	Coleraine	Coleraine	Irish Society
Coleraine, Russell Terrace	Coleraine	Killowen	Coleraine	Coleraine	Churchland
Coleraine, Sandy Row	Coleraine	Coleraine	Coleraine	Coleraine	Irish Society
Coleraine, Shanbles Fish Market	Coleraine	Coleraine	Coleraine	Coleraine	Irish Society
Coleraine, Shuttle Hill	Coleraine	Killowen	Coleraine	Coleraine	Churchland
Coleraine, Society Street	Coleraine	Coleraine	Coleraine	Coleraine	Irish Society
Coleraine, Spittle Hill Gardens	Coleraine	Coleraine	Coleraine	Coleraine	Irish Society
Coleraine, Stable Lane	Coleraine	Coleraine	Coleraine	Coleraine	Irish Society
Coleraine, Stone Row Lower	Coleraine	Coleraine	Coleraine	Coleraine	Irish Society
Coleraine, Stone Row Upper	Coleraine	Coleraine	Coleraine	Coleraine	Irish Society
Coleraine, Strand Road Lower	Coleraine	Killowen	Coleraine	Coleraine	Churchland
Coleraine, Strand Road Upper	Coleraine	Killowen	Coleraine	Coleraine	Churchland
Coleraine, Taylors Row	Coleraine	Coleraine	Coleraine	Coleraine	Irish Society
Coleraine, Terrace Row	Coleraine	Coleraine	Coleraine	Coleraine	Irish Society
Coleraine, The Diamond	Coleraine	Coleraine	Coleraine	Coleraine	Irish Society
Coleraine, Union Street	Coleraine	Coleraine	Coleraine	Coleraine	Irish Society
Coleraine, Victoria Terrace	Coleraine	Coleraine	Coleraine	Coleraine	Irish Society
Coleraine, Waterford Place	Coleraine	Coleraine	Coleraine	Coleraine	Irish Society
Coleraine, Waterford Terrace	Coleraine	Coleraine	Coleraine	Coleraine	Irish Society
Coleraine, Waterside Street	Coleraine	Killowen	Coleraine	Coleraine	Churchland
Coleraine, Waterside Street	Coleraine	Killowen	Coleraine	Coleraine	Churchland
Coleraine, Waverly Terrace	Coleraine	Coleraine	Coleraine	Coleraine	Irish Society
Collins	Drumcroon	Aghadowey	Aghadowey	Coleraine	Ironmongers
Coltrim	Moneymore	Lissan	Moneymore	Magherafelt	Drapers
Coney Island	Castle Dawson	Ballyscullion	Bellaghy	Magherafelt	Phillips

Townland	D.E.D.	Parish	Registrar District	Poor Law Union	17th Century Landowner
Coolafinny	Eglinton	Faughanvale	Eglinton	Londonderry	Grocers
Coolagh	Faughanvale	Faughanvale	Ballykelly	Limavady	Churchland
Coolcoscreaghan	Slaght	Errigal	Garvagh	Coleraine	Ironmongers
Coolderry North	Knockantern	Kildollagh	Coleraine	Coleraine	Irish Society
Coolderry South	Knockantern	Kildollagh	Coleraine	Coleraine	Irish Society
Coole Glebe Lower	Somerset	Macosquin	Aghadowey	Coleraine	Churchland
Coole Glebe Upper	Somerset	Macosquin	Aghadowey	Coleraine	Churchland
Coolessan	Fruithill	Drumachose	Limavady	Limavady	Phillips
Coolhill	Kilrea	Aghadowey	Kilrea	Coleraine	Mercers
Coolkeenaght	Faughanvale	Faughanvale	Ballykelly	Limavady	Fishmongers
Coolkeeragh	Lough Enagh	Clondermot	Eglinton	Londonderry	Grocers
Coolnacolpagh	Foreglen	Cumber Upper	Feeny	Limavady	Fishmongers
Coolnamonan	Feeny	Banagher	Feeny	Limavady	Skinners
Coolnasillagh	Carnamoney	Ballynascreen	Draperstown	Magherafelt	Drapers
Coolnasillagh	Glenkeen	Errigal	Garvagh	Coleraine	Ironmongers
Coolsaragh	Iniscarn	Kilcronaghan	Draperstown	Magherafelt	Drapers
Coolshinny	Ballymoghan	Magherafelt	Magherafelt	Magherafelt	Salters
Coolyvenny	Somerset	Macosquin	Aghadowey	Coleraine	Merchant Taylors
Corick	Bancran	Ballynascreen	Draperstown	Magherafelt	Churchland
Corick	Glenshane	Dungiven	Dungiven	Limavady	Skinners
Corlacky	Swatragh	Killelagh	Maghera	Magherafelt	Vintners
Cornamuclagh	Agivey	Aghadowey	Aghadowey	Coleraine	Ironmongers
Corndale Lower	Myroe	Tamlaght Finlagan	Bellarena	Limavady	Phillips
Corndale Upper	Myroe	Tamlaght Finlagan	Bellarena	Limavady	Phillips
Corrody	Glendermot	Clondermot	Waterside Rural	Londonderry	Goldsmiths
Corrstown	Ballylagan	Ballywillin	Portstewart	Coleraine	Irish Society
Coshquin	Liberties Lower	Templemore	Liberties Lower	Londonderry	Irish Society
Crabarkey	Glenshane	Dungiven	Dungiven	Limavady	Skinners
Craig	Benone	Magilligan	Bellarena	Limavady	Churchland
Craigadick	Maghera	Maghera	Maghera	Magherafelt	Churchland
Craigall	Bovagh	Desertoghill	Garvagh	Coleraine	Ironmongers
Craigavole	The Grove	Desertoghill	Kilrea	Coleraine	Mercers
Craigbrack	Eglinton	Faughanvale	Eglinton	Londonderry	Grocers
Craiglea Glebe	Aghadowey	Aghadowey	Aghadowey	Coleraine	Churchland
Craigmore	Ringsend	Aghadowey	Aghadowey	Coleraine	Merchant Taylors
Craigmore	Maghera	Maghera	Maghera	Magherafelt	Churchland
Craignahorn	Ballylagan	Ballywillin	Portstewart	Coleraine	Irish Society
Craigtown	Glendermot	Clondermot	Waterside Rural	Londonderry	Goldsmiths
Craigtown Beg	Portstewart	Ballyaghran	Portstewart	Coleraine	Irish Society
Craigtown More	Portstewart	Ballyaghran	Portstewart	Coleraine	Irish Society

Townland	D.E.D.	Parish	Registrar District	Poor Law Union	17th Century Landowner
Cranny	Brackagh Slieve Gallion	Desertmartin	Moneymore	Magherafelt	Drapers
Creevagh Lower	Liberties Upper	Templemore	Liberties Upper	Londonderry	Irish Society
Creevagh Upper	Liberties Upper	Templemore	Liberties Upper	Londonderry	Irish Society
Creevedonnell	Glendermot	Clondermot	Waterside Rural	Londonderry	Goldsmiths
Cregan	Eglinton	Faughanvale	Eglinton	Londonderry	Grocers
Cregg	Claudy	Cumber Upper	Claudy	Londonderry	Churchland
Creggan	Londonderry Urban No. 1	Templemore	Londonderry Urban No. 2	Londonderry	Churchland
Creggan	Liberties Upper	Templemore	Liberties Upper	Londonderry	Churchland
Cressy Crib	Myroe	Aghanloo	Bellarena	Limavady	Haberdashers
Crevolea	Aghadowey	Aghadowey	Aghadowey	Coleraine	Churchland
Crew	Maghera	Maghera	Maghera	Magherafelt	Churchland
Crindle	Myroe	Tamlaght Finlagan	Bellarena	Limavady	Phillips
Crindle village	Myroe	Tamlaght Finlagan	Bellarena	Limavady	Phillips
Croaghan	Letterloan	Macosquin	Articlave	Coleraine	Merchant Taylors
Croaghan	Bellarena	Magilligan	Bellarena	Limavady	Churchland
Crockindollagh	Glenkeen	Errigal	Garvagh	Coleraine	Ironmongers
Cromkill	Ardmore	Clondermot	Waterside Rural	Londonderry	Churchland
Cross Glebe	Knockantern	Coleraine	Coleraine	Coleraine	Irish Society
Crossballycormick	Tamnaherin	Cumber Lower	Eglinton	Londonderry	Goldsmiths
Crosscanley Glebe	Drumcroon	Aghadowey	Aghadowey	Coleraine	Churchland
Crossgar	Drumcroon	Macosquin	Aghadowey	Coleraine	Merchant Taylors
Crossland	The Grove	Desertoghill	Kilrea	Coleraine	Mercers
Crossmakeever	Letterloan	Aghadowey	Articlave	Coleraine	Merchant Taylors
Crossnarea	Moneymore	Desertlyn	Moneymore	Magherafelt	Churchland
Crossreagh	Ballylagan	Ballywillin	Portstewart	Coleraine	Irish Society
Crossreagh East	Portstewart	Ballyaghran	Portstewart	Coleraine	Irish Society
Crossreagh West	Portstewart	Ballyaghran	Portstewart	Coleraine	Irish Society
Cruckanim	Glenshane	Dungiven	Dungiven	Limavady	Skinners
Cuilbane	Slaght	Desertoghill	Garvagh	Coleraine	Ironmongers
Culcrow	Agivey	Agivey	Aghadowey	Coleraine	Ironmongers
Culdrum	Drumcroon	Aghadowey	Aghadowey	Coleraine	Ironmongers
Culdrum	Drumcroon	Macosquin	Aghadowey	Coleraine	Ironmongers
Cullion	Iniscarn	Desertmartin	Draperstown	Magherafelt	Drapers
Cullycapple	Agivey	Aghadowey	Aghadowey	Coleraine	Ironmongers
Cullyramer	Bovagh	Aghadowey	Garvagh	Coleraine	Ironmongers
Cullyramer	Bovagh	Desertoghill	Garvagh	Coleraine	Ironmongers
Culmore	Liberties Lower	Templemore	Liberties Lower	Londonderry	Irish Society
Culmore Level	Liberties Lower	Templemore	Liberties Lower	Londonderry	Irish Society
Culmore Lower	Myroe	Tamlaght Finlagan	Bellarena	Limavady	Phillips

Townland	D.E.D.	Parish	Registrar District	Poor Law Union	17th Century Landowner
Culmore Upper	The Highlands	Tamlaght Finlagan	Ballykelly	Limavady	Phillips
Culnady	Maghera	Maghera	Maghera	Magherafelt	Vintners
Culnagrew	Swatragh	Killelagh	Maghera	Magherafelt	Mercers
Culnaman	Bovagh	Desertoghill	Garvagh	Coleraine	Ironmongers
Cumber	Claudy	Cumber Upper	Claudy	Londonderry	Churchland
Curr	Desertmartin	Desertmartin	Magherafelt	Magherafelt	Churchland
Curragh	Somerset	Macosquin	Aghadowey	Coleraine	Merchant Taylors
Curragh	Gulladuff	Maghera	Maghera	Magherafelt	Vintners
Curraghlane	Dungiven	Dungiven	Dungiven	Limavady	Skinners
Curran	Desertmartin	Maghera	Magherafelt	Magherafelt	Vintners
Curran town	Desertmartin	Maghera	Magherafelt	Magherafelt	Vintners
Currudda	Glenshane	Dungiven	Dungiven	Limavady	Skinners
Curryfree	Glendermot	Clondermot	Waterside Rural	Londonderry	Goldsmiths
Currynierin	Ardmore	Clondermot	Waterside Rural	Londonderry	Grocers
Damhead	Knockantern	Kildollagh	Coleraine	Coleraine	Irish Society
Danes Hill	Ballylagan	Coleraine	Portstewart	Coleraine	Irish Society
Dartress	Articlave	Dunboe	Articlave	Coleraine	Clothworkers
Deer Park	Fruithill	Drumachose	Limavady	Limavady	Phillips
Deer Park	The Highlands	Tamlaght Finlagan	Ballykelly	Limavady	Phillips
Derganagh	Rocktown	Termoneeny	Bellaghy	Magherafelt	Vintners
Dernagross	Aghadowey	Aghadowey	Aghadowey	Coleraine	Churchland
Derryard	Drum	Bovevagh	Dungiven	Limavady	Phillips
Derryarkin Lower	Eglinton	Faughanvale	Eglinton	Londonderry	Grocers
Derryarkin Upper	Eglinton	Faughanvale	Eglinton	Londonderry	Grocers
Derrybeg	Fruithill	Drumachose	Limavady	Limavady	Phillips
Derrychrier	Owenreagh	Banagher	Feeny	Limavady	Churchland
Derrycrummy	Moneyhaw	Derryloran	Moneymore	Magherafelt	Drapers
Derrydorragh	Drumcroon	Macosquin	Aghadowey	Coleraine	Merchant Taylors
Derryduff	Dungiven	Dungiven	Dungiven	Limavady	Skinners
Derryganard	Lissan Upper	Lissan	Moneymore	Magherafelt	Churchland
Derrygarve	Castle Dawson	Artrea	Bellaghy	Magherafelt	Phillips
Derrylane	Drum	Bovevagh	Dungiven	Limavady	Phillips
Derrymore	Fruithill	Drumachose	Limavady	Limavady	Phillips
Derrynaflaw	Drum	Bovevagh	Dungiven	Limavady	Phillips
Derrynoyd	Draperstown	Ballynascreen	Draperstown	Magherafelt	Skinners
Derryork Large	Gelvin	Dungiven	Dungiven	Limavady	Haberdashers
Derryork Small	Gelvin	Bovevagh	Dungiven	Limavady	Haberdashers
Derryware	Dungiven	Dungiven	Dungiven	Limavady	Skinners
Desertmartin town	Desertmartin	Desertmartin	Magherafelt	Magherafelt	Churchland
Dirnan	Lissan Upper	Lissan	Moneymore	Magherafelt	Churchland
Dirtagh	Aghanloo	Aghanloo	Bellarena	Limavady	Haberdashers

Townland	D.E.D.	Parish	Registrar District	Poor Law Union	17th Century Landowner
Disert	Bancran	Ballynascreen	Draperstown	Magherafelt	Skinners
Disertowen	Glendermot	Clondermot	Waterside Rural	Londonderry	Goldsmiths
Doaghs Lower	Benone	Magilligan	Bellarena	Limavady	Churchland
Doaghs Lower Middle	Benone	Magilligan	Bellarena	Limavady	Churchland
Doaghs Upper	Benone	Magilligan	Bellarena	Limavady	Churchland
Doaghs Upper Middle	Benone	Magilligan	Bellarena	Limavady	Churchland
Doluskey	Moneymore	Artrea	Moneymore	Magherafelt	Salters
Donnybrewer	Eglinton	Faughanvale	Eglinton	Londonderry	Grocers
Donnybrewer Level	Eglinton	Faughanvale	Eglinton	Londonderry	Grocers
Dooey Beg	Portstewart	Ballyaghran	Portstewart	Coleraine	Irish Society
Doon	Bancran	Ballynascreen	Draperstown	Magherafelt	Skinners
Dowland	Aghanloo	Aghanloo	Bellarena	Limavady	Haberdashers
Downhill	Downhill	Dunboe	Articlave	Coleraine	Churchland
Draperstown town	Draperstown	Ballynascreen	Draperstown	Magherafelt	Drapers
Dreen	Banagher	Learmount	Claudy	Londonderry	Skinners
Dreenan	Gulladuff	Maghera	Maghera	Magherafelt	Vintners
Droghed	Agivey	Aghadowey	Aghadowey	Coleraine	Ironmongers
Dromore	Desertmartin	Desertmartin	Magherafelt	Magherafelt	Churchland
Dromore	Knockantern	Kildollagh	Coleraine	Coleraine	Irish Society
Dromore	Drumcroon	Macosquin	Aghadowey	Coleraine	Merchant Taylors
Dromore	The Highlands	Tamlaght Finlagan	Ballykelly	Limavady	Phillips
Drum	Drum	Bovevagh	Dungiven	Limavady	Phillips
Drumacarney	Ballykelly	Tamlaght Finlagan	Ballykelly	Limavady	Phillips
Drumacony	Ballykelly	Tamlaght Finlagan	Ballykelly	Limavady	Fishmongers
Drumacrow	Aghadowey	Aghadowey	Aghadowey	Coleraine	Churchland
Drumaderry	Aghanloo	Aghanloo	Bellarena	Limavady	Haberdashers
Drumadragh	Ballylagan	Coleraine	Portstewart	Coleraine	Irish Society
Drumadreen	Gelvin	Bovevagh	Dungiven	Limavady	Haberdashers
Drumaduan	Knockantern	Kildollagh	Coleraine	Coleraine	Irish Society
Drumaduff	Gelvin	Bovevagh	Dungiven	Limavady	Haberdashers
Drumagarner	Hervey Hill	Tamlaght O'Crilly	Kilrea	Coleraine	Churchland
Drumagore	Glendermot	Clondermot	Waterside Rural	Londonderry	Goldsmiths
Drumagosker	Lislane	Balteagh	Limavady	Limavady	Haberdashers
Drumagully	Downhill	Dunboe	Articlave	Coleraine	Churchland
Drumahoe	Waterside	Clondermot	Waterside Rural	Londonderry	Goldsmiths
Drumahorgan	Benone	Magilligan	Bellarena	Limavady	Churchland
Drumalief	Aghanloo	Aghanloo	Bellarena	Limavady	Haberdashers
Drumane	Hervey Hill	Tamlaght O'Crilly	Kilrea	Coleraine	Churchland

Townland	D.E.D.	Parish	Registrar District	Poor Law Union	17th Century Landowner
Drumanee Lower	Bellaghy	Ballyscullion	Bellaghy	Magherafelt	Vintners
Drumanee Upper	Bellaghy	Ballyscullion	Bellaghy	Magherafelt	Vintners
Drumaquill	Bannbrook	Killowen	Articlave	Coleraine	Clothworkers
Drumard	Draperstown	Ballynascreen	Draperstown	Magherafelt	Skinners
Drumard	Lissan Upper	Lissan	Moneymore	Magherafelt	Churchland
Drumard	Rocktown	Maghera	Bellaghy	Magherafelt	Vintners
Drumard	Tamlaght	Tamlaght O'Crilly	Kilrea	Coleraine	Churchland
Drumavally	Bellarena	Magilligan	Bellarena	Limavady	Churchland
Drumballydonaghy	Fruithill	Tamlaght Finlagan	Limavady	Limavady	Phillips
Drumballyhagan	Tobermore	Kilcronaghan	Maghera	Magherafelt	Vintners
Drumballyhagan Clark	Tobermore	Kilcronaghan	Maghera	Magherafelt	Vintners
Drumbane	Aghanloo	Aghanloo	Bellarena	Limavady	Churchland
Drumbane	Slaght	Errigal	Garvagh	Coleraine	Ironmongers
Drumconan	Glendermot	Clondermot	Waterside Rural	Londonderry	Goldsmiths
Drumconready	Carnamoney	Maghera	Draperstown	Magherafelt	Drapers
Drumcovit	Feeny	Banagher	Feeny	Limavady	Fishmongers
Drumcroon	Drumcroon	Macosquin	Aghadowey	Coleraine	Ironmongers
Drumcrow	Tobermore	Kilcronaghan	Maghera	Magherafelt	Vintners
Drumderg	Draperstown	Ballynascreen	Draperstown	Magherafelt	Skinners
Drumeil	Agivey	Aghadowey	Aghadowey	Coleraine	Ironmongers
Drumenagh	Ballyronan	Artrea	Magherafelt	Magherafelt	Salters
Drumgavenny Lower	Lislane	Balteagh	Limavady	Limavady	Haberdashers
Drumgavenny Upper	Lislane	Balteagh	Limavady	Limavady	Haberdashers
Drumgesh	Fruithill	Balteagh	Limavady	Limavady	Churchland
Druminard	Salterstown	Tamlaght	Magherafelt	Magherafelt	Salters
Drumlamph	Rocktown	Maghera	Bellaghy	Magherafelt	Vintners
Drumlane	Tamlaght	Tamlaght O'Crilly	Kilrea	Coleraine	Churchland
Drummaneny	Eglinton	Faughanvale	Eglinton	Londonderry	Grocers
Drummans Lower	Benone	Magilligan	Bellarena	Limavady	Churchland
Drummans Middle	Benone	Magilligan	Bellarena	Limavady	Churchland
Drummans Upper	Benone	Magilligan	Bellarena	Limavady	Churchland
Drummeen	Moneymore	Lissan	Moneymore	Magherafelt	Churchland
Drummeen (No. 2)	Moneymore	Lissan	Moneymore	Magherafelt	Drapers
Drummond	Fruithill	Drumachose	Limavady	Limavady	Churchland
Drummond	Ballykelly	Tamlaght Finlagan	Ballykelly	Limavady	Fishmongers
Drummuck	Gulladuff	Maghera	Maghera	Magherafelt	Mercers
Drummullan	Springhill	Arboe	Moneymore	Magherafelt	Churchland
Drumnacanon	Tamlaght	Tamlaght O'Crilly	Kilrea	Coleraine	Churchland
Drumnahay	Bellarena	Magilligan	Bellarena	Limavady	Churchland

Townland	D.E.D.	Parish	Registrar District	Poor Law Union	17th Century Landowner
Drumneechy	Gelvin	Bovevagh	Dungiven	Limavady	Haberdashers
Drumoolish	Tamlaght	Tamlaght O'Crilly	Kilrea	Coleraine	Churchland
Drumraighland	The Highlands	Tamlaght Finlagan	Ballykelly	Limavady	Phillips
Drumrainey	Magherafelt	Magherafelt	Magherafelt	Magherafelt	Salters
Drumramer	Keady	Drumachose	Limavady	Limavady	Merchant Taylors
Drumrane	The Highlands	Tamlaght Finlagan	Ballykelly	Limavady	Phillips
Drumrot	Moneyhaw	Derryloran	Moneymore	Magherafelt	Drapers
Drumrot	Moneyhaw	Lissan	Moneymore	Magherafelt	Drapers
Drumsamney	Tobermore	Kilcronaghan	Maghera	Magherafelt	Churchland
Drumsaragh	Hervey Hill	Tamlaght O'Crilly	Kilrea	Coleraine	Mercers
Drumslade	Portstewart	Ballyaghran	Portstewart	Coleraine	Irish Society
Drumsteeple	Agivey	Aghadowey	Aghadowey	Coleraine	Ironmongers
Drumsurn Lower	Lislane	Balteagh	Limavady	Limavady	Haberdashers
Drumsurn Upper	Lislane	Balteagh	Limavady	Limavady	Haberdashers
Dullaghy	The Grove	Desertoghill	Kilrea	Coleraine	Mercers
Dunady	Ballymullins	Cumber Upper	Claudy	Londonderry	Skinners
Dunalis Lower	Articlave	Dunboe	Articlave	Coleraine	Clothworkers
Dunalis Upper	Articlave	Dunboe	Articlave	Coleraine	Clothworkers
Dunamoney	Magherafelt	Magherafelt	Magherafelt	Magherafelt	Salters
Dunarnon	Ballymoghan	Magherafelt	Magherafelt	Magherafelt	Salters
Dunbeg	Keady	Drumachose	Limavady	Limavady	Churchland
Dunbrock	Ballykelly	Tamlaght Finlagan	Ballykelly	Limavady	Fishmongers
Duncrun	Bellarena	Magilligan	Bellarena	Limavady	Churchland
Dunderg	Drumcroon	Macosquin	Aghadowey	Coleraine	Merchant Taylors
Dundooan	Ballylagan	Ballyaghran	Portstewart	Coleraine	Irish Society
Dundooan	Ballylagan	Ballywillin	Portstewart	Coleraine	Irish Society
Dundooan	Ballylagan	Coleraine	Portstewart	Coleraine	Irish Society
Dungiven	Dungiven	Dungiven	Dungiven	Limavady	Skinners
Dungiven town	Dungiven	Dungiven	Dungiven	Limavady	Skinners
Dunglady	Swatragh	Maghera	Maghera	Magherafelt	Mercers
Dungorkin	Foreglen	Cumber Upper	Feeny	Limavady	Fishmongers
Dungullion	Faughanvale	Faughanvale	Ballykelly	Limavady	Fishmongers
Dunhugh	Glendermot	Clondermot	Waterside Rural	Londonderry	Goldsmiths
Dunlade Glebe	Faughanvale	Faughanvale	Ballykelly	Limavady	Churchland
Dunlogan	Draperstown	Ballynascreen	Draperstown	Magherafelt	Drapers
Dunman	Moneyhaw	Derryloran	Moneymore	Magherafelt	Drapers
Dunmore	Keady	Drumachose	Limavady	Limavady	Churchland
Dunmurry	Carnamoney	Ballynascreen	Draperstown	Magherafelt	Drapers
Dunnabraggy	Moneyhaw	Lissan	Moneymore	Magherafelt	Drapers

Townland	D.E.D.	Parish	Registrar District	Poor Law Union	17th Century Landowner
Dunnavenny	Slaght	Errigal	Garvagh	Coleraine	Ironmongers
Dunronan	Ballymoghan	Desertlyn	Magherafelt	Magherafelt	Salters
Duntibryan	Carnamoney	Ballynascreen	Draperstown	Magherafelt	Drapers
Durnascallon	Brackagh Slieve Gallion	Desertmartin	Moneymore	Magherafelt	Drapers
Eden	Glenshane	Dungiven	Dungiven	Limavady	Skinners
Eden	Banagher	Learmount	Claudy	Londonderry	Skinners
Eden	Clady	Tamlaght O'Crilly	Bellaghy	Magherafelt	Vintners
Edenballymore	Londonderry Urban No. 1	Templemore	Londonderry Urban No. 2	Londonderry	Churchland
Edenbane	Garvagh	Desertoghill	Garvagh	Coleraine	Ironmongers
Edenmore	Fruithill	Balteagh	Limavady	Limavady	Churchland
Edenreagh	Bellaghy	Ballyscullion	Bellaghy	Magherafelt	Phillips
Edenreagh Beg	Lough Enagh	Clondermot	Eglinton	Londonderry	Grocers
Edenreagh More	Lough Enagh	Clondermot	Eglinton	Londonderry	Grocers
Elagh More	Liberties Lower	Templemore	Liberties Lower	Londonderry	Irish Society
Enagh	Lough Enagh	Clondermot	Eglinton	Londonderry	Churchland
Enagh	Fruithill	Drumachose	Limavady	Limavady	Churchland
Englishtown	Somerset	Macosquin	Aghadowey	Coleraine	Merchant Taylors
Erganagh	Kilrea	Kilrea	Kilrea	Coleraine	Mercers
Ervey	Tamnaherin	Cumber Lower	Eglinton	Londonderry	Grocers
Evishagaran	Glenshane	Dungiven	Dungiven	Limavady	Skinners
Exorna	Articlave	Dunboe	Articlave	Coleraine	Clothworkers
Falgortrevy	Maghera	Maghera	Maghera	Magherafelt	Churchland
Fallagloon	Tullykeeran	Maghera	Maghera	Magherafelt	Vintners
Fallahogy	Tamlaght	Kilrea	Kilrea	Coleraine	Mercers
Falloward	Eglinton	Faughanvale	Eglinton	Londonderry	Grocers
Fallowlea	Eglinton	Faughanvale	Eglinton	Londonderry	Grocers
Fallylea	Tullykeeran	Killelagh	Maghera	Magherafelt	Vintners
Farkland	Drum	Bovevagh	Dungiven	Limavady	Skinners
Farlow	Myroe	Tamlaght Finlagan	Bellarena	Limavady	Fishmongers
Farranlester	Bannbrook	Dunboe	Articlave	Coleraine	Churchland
Farranlester	Somerset	Macosquin	Aghadowey	Coleraine	Merchant Taylors
Farranseer	Drumcroon	Macosquin	Aghadowey	Coleraine	Merchant Taylors
Farrantemple Glebe	Slaght	Errigal	Garvagh	Coleraine	Churchland
Faughanvale	Faughanvale	Faughanvale	Ballykelly	Limavady	Churchland
Fawney	Tamnaherin	Cumber Lower	Eglinton	Londonderry	Goldsmiths
Feenan Beg	Moneymore	Desertlyn	Moneymore	Magherafelt	Churchland
Feenan More	Moneymore	Desertlyn	Moneymore	Magherafelt	Churchland
Feeny	Feeny	Banagher	Feeny	Limavady	Fishmongers
Feeny town	Feeny	Banagher	Feeny	Limavady	Fishmongers

Townland	D.E.D.	Parish	Registrar District	Poor Law Union	17th Century Landowner
Fincarn	Feeny	Banagher	Feeny	Limavady	Skinners
Fincarn	Waterside	Clondermot	Waterside Rural	Londonderry	Goldsmiths
Finglen	Draperstown	Ballynascreen	Draperstown	Magherafelt	Drapers
Finglen	Owenreagh	Banagher	Feeny	Limavady	Churchland
Fish Loughan	Knockantern	Kildollagh	Coleraine	Coleraine	Irish Society
Flanders	Drum	Bovevagh	Dungiven	Limavady	Phillips
Formil	Gelvin	Bovevagh	Dungiven	Limavady	Haberdashers
Formoyle	Articlave	Formoyle	Articlave	Coleraine	Clothworkers
Formullen	Articlave	Formoyle	Articlave	Coleraine	Clothworkers
Freehall Dunlop	Downhill	Dunboe	Articlave	Coleraine	Clothworkers
Freehall or Moneyvennon	Aghanloo	Aghanloo	Bellarena	Limavady	Haberdashers
Freehall Watson	Downhill	Dunboe	Articlave	Coleraine	Clothworkers
Freugh	Ringsend	Errigal	Aghadowey	Coleraine	Merchant Taylors
Fruithill	Fruithill	Drumachose	Limavady	Limavady	Churchland
Gallany	Feeny	Banagher	Feeny	Limavady	Skinners
Galvally	Portstewart	Ballyaghran	Portstewart	Coleraine	Irish Society
Garborgle	Portstewart	Ballyaghran	Portstewart	Coleraine	Irish Society
Garrylaban	Portstewart	Ballyaghran	Portstewart	Coleraine	Irish Society
Garvagh	Garvagh	Errigal	Garvagh	Coleraine	Ironmongers
Garvagh town	Garvagh	Errigal	Garvagh	Coleraine	Ironmongers
Gateside	Ballylagan	Coleraine	Portstewart	Coleraine	Irish Society
Gilky Hill	Claudy	Cumber Upper	Claudy	Londonderry	Churchland
Gills	Somerset	Macosquin	Aghadowey	Coleraine	Merchant Taylors
Glack	Ballykelly	Tamlaght Finlagan	Ballykelly	Limavady	Fishmongers
Glasakeeran	Faughanvale	Faughanvale	Ballykelly	Limavady	Fishmongers
Glasgort	Agivey	Agivey	Aghadowey	Coleraine	Ironmongers
Glasvey	Ballykelly	Tamlaght Finlagan	Ballykelly	Limavady	Fishmongers
Glebe	Aghanloo	Aghanloo	Bellarena	Limavady	Churchland
Glebe	Portstewart	Ballyaghran	Portstewart	Coleraine	Irish Society
Glebe	Draperstown	Ballynascreen	Draperstown	Magherafelt	Churchland
Glebe	Knockantern	Ballyrashane	Coleraine	Coleraine	Irish Society
Glebe	Ballylagan	Ballywillin	Portstewart	Coleraine	Irish Society
Glebe	Fruithill	Balteagh	Limavady	Limavady	Churchland
Glebe	Gelvin	Bovevagh	Dungiven	Limavady	Churchland
Glebe	Keady	Drumachose	Limavady	Limavady	Churchland
Glebe	Faughanvale	Faughanvale	Ballykelly	Limavady	Churchland
Glebe	Tullykeeran	Killelagh	Maghera	Magherafelt	Churchland
Glebe	Lissan Upper	Lissan	Moneymore	Magherafelt	Churchland
Glebe	Magherafelt	Magherafelt	Magherafelt	Magherafelt	Churchland
Glebe	Bellarena	Magilligan	Bellarena	Limavady	Churchland

Townland	D.E.D.	Parish	Registrar District	Poor Law Union	17th Century Landowner
Glebe	Ballykelly	Tamlaght Finlagan	Ballykelly	Limavady	Churchland
Glebe East	Bellaghy	Ballyscullion	Bellaghy	Magherafelt	Churchland
Glebe West	Bellaghy	Ballyscullion	Bellaghy	Magherafelt	Churchland
Glenback	Agivey	Aghadowey	Aghadowey	Coleraine	Ironmongers
Glenconway	Straw	Bovevagh	Ballykelly	Limavady	Phillips
Glencurb	Ringsend	Aghadowey	Aghadowey	Coleraine	Merchant Taylors
Glenderowen	Glendermot	Clondermot	Waterside Rural	Londonderry	Goldsmiths
Glenedra	Owenreagh	Banagher	Feeny	Limavady	Churchland
Glengomna	Bancran	Ballynascreen	Draperstown	Magherafelt	Skinners
Glenhall	Somerset	Macosquin	Aghadowey	Coleraine	Merchant Taylors
Glenkeen	Agivey	Aghadowey	Aghadowey	Coleraine	Ironmongers
Glenkeen	Ardmore	Clondermot	Waterside Rural	Londonderry	Grocers
Glenkeen	Keady	Drumachose	Limavady	Limavady	Merchant Taylors
Glenkeen	Glenkeen	Errigal	Garvagh	Coleraine	Ironmongers
Glenleary	Somerset	Macosquin	Aghadowey	Coleraine	Merchant Taylors
Glenlough	Bondsglen	Cumber Upper	Claudy	Londonderry	Skinners
Glenmanus	Ballylagan	Ballywillin	Portstewart	Coleraine	Irish Society
Glenmaquill	Desertmartin	Magherafelt	Magherafelt	Magherafelt	Vintners
Glenone	Clady	Tamlaght O'Crilly	Bellaghy	Magherafelt	Vintners
Glenshane	Glenshane	Dungiven	Dungiven	Limavady	Skinners
Glenviggan	The Six Towns	Ballynascreen	Draperstown	Magherafelt	Churchland
Gobnascale	Waterside	Clondermot	Waterside Rural	Londonderry	Goldsmiths
Gobnascale	Waterside	Clondermot	Waterside Urban	Londonderry	Goldsmiths
Gorran	Aghadowey	Aghadowey	Aghadowey	Coleraine	Churchland
Gort	Garvagh	Desertoghill	Garvagh	Coleraine	Churchland
Gort	Bellarena	Magilligan	Bellarena	Limavady	Churchland
Gortaclare	Gelvin	Bovevagh	Dungiven	Limavady	Haberdashers
Gortacloghan	Slaght	Desertoghill	Garvagh	Coleraine	Ironmongers
Gortagherty Lower	Eglinton	Faughanvale	Eglinton	Londonderry	Grocers
Gortagherty Upper	Eglinton	Faughanvale	Eglinton	Londonderry	Grocers
Gortagilly	Ballymoghan	Desertlyn	Magherafelt	Magherafelt	Salters
Gortahurk	Iniscarn	Kilcronaghan	Draperstown	Magherafelt	Drapers
Gortamney	Tobermore	Kilcronaghan	Maghera	Magherafelt	Drapers
Gortanewry	Brackagh Slieve Gallion	Desertmartin	Moneymore	Magherafelt	Drapers
Gortcorbies	Keady	Drumachose	Limavady	Limavady	Haberdashers
Gorteade	Swatragh	Maghera	Maghera	Magherafelt	Mercers
Gortenny	Eglinton	Faughanvale	Eglinton	Londonderry	Grocers
Gortfad	Glenkeen	Errigal	Garvagh	Coleraine	Ironmongers
Gortgare	Faughanvale	Faughanvale	Ballykelly	Limavady	Fishmongers

Townland	D.E.D.	Parish	Registrar District	Poor Law Union	17th Century Landowner
Gortgarn	Keady	Drumachose	Limavady	Limavady	Haberdashers
Gortgarn	Gelvin	Dungiven	Dungiven	Limavady	Haberdashers
Gortgran	Bannbrook	Dunboe	Articlave	Coleraine	Churchland
Gortgranagh	Glendermot	Clondermot	Waterside Rural	Londonderry	Grocers
Gortica	Waterside	Clondermot	Waterside Rural	Londonderry	Goldsmiths
Gorticloghan	Knockantern	Ballyrashane	Coleraine	Coleraine	Irish Society
Gorticross	Lough Enagh	Clondermot	Eglinton	Londonderry	Grocers
Gortilea	Foreglen	Cumber Upper	Feeny	Limavady	Fishmongers
Gortin	Glendermot	Clondermot	Waterside Rural	Londonderry	Goldsmiths
Gortin Coolhill	Kilrea	Aghadowey	Kilrea	Coleraine	Mercers
Gortin Mayoghill	Bovagh	Aghadowey	Garvagh	Coleraine	Ironmongers
Gortinreid	Tamnaherin	Cumber Lower	Eglinton	Londonderry	Grocers
Gortinure	Glendermot	Clondermot	Waterside Rural	Londonderry	Goldsmiths
Gortinure	Tullykeeran	Killelagh	Maghera	Magherafelt	Churchland
Gortmacrane	Hervey Hill	Tamlaght O'Crilly	Kilrea	Coleraine	Churchland
Gortmore	Benone	Magilligan	Bellarena	Limavady	Churchland
Gortnagross	Gelvin	Dungiven	Dungiven	Limavady	Haberdashers
Gortnahey Beg	Drum	Bovevagh	Dungiven	Limavady	Phillips
Gortnahey More	Drum	Bovevagh	Dungiven	Limavady	Phillips
Gortnamoney	Aghanloo	Aghanloo	Bellarena	Limavady	Haberdashers
Gortnamoyagh	Glenkeen	Errigal	Garvagh	Coleraine	Churchland
Gortnaran	Bondsglen	Cumber Upper	Claudy	Londonderry	Skinners
Gortnarney	Lislane	Balteagh	Limavady	Limavady	Haberdashers
Gortnaskey	Draperstown	Ballynascreen	Draperstown	Magherafelt	Drapers
Gortnaskey	Bondsglen	Cumber Upper	Claudy	Londonderry	Skinners
Gortnessy	Lough Enagh	Clondermot	Eglinton	Londonderry	Grocers
Gortree	Lough Enagh	Clondermot	Eglinton	Londonderry	Goldsmiths
Gortscreagan	Ballymullins	Learmount	Claudy	Londonderry	Fishmongers
Gortycavan	Articlave	Dunboe	Articlave	Coleraine	Clothworkers
Gosheden	Ardmore	Cumber Lower	Waterside Rural	Londonderry	Grocers
Granaghan	Swatragh	Killelagh	Maghera	Magherafelt	Mercers
Grange	Desertmartin	Desertmartin	Magherafelt	Magherafelt	Vintners
Grange Beg	Bannbrook	Dunboe	Articlave	Coleraine	Churchland
Grange More	Bannbrook	Dunboe	Articlave	Coleraine	Churchland
Grange More Upper	Bannbrook	Dunboe	Articlave	Coleraine	Churchland
Grange Park	Aghanloo	Aghanloo	Bellarena	Limavady	Haberdashers
Grannagh	Aghanloo	Aghanloo	Bellarena	Limavady	Haberdashers
Granny	Tobermore	Kilcronaghan	Maghera	Magherafelt	Churchland
Gransha	Lough Enagh	Clondermot	Eglinton	Londonderry	Churchland
Gransha Intake	Lough Enagh	Clondermot	Eglinton	Londonderry	Churchland
Greenan	Lough Enagh	Faughanvale	Eglinton	Londonderry	Grocers
Gresteel Beg	Faughanvale	Faughanvale	Ballykelly	Limavady	Fishmongers

33

Townland	D.E.D.	Parish	Registrar District	Poor Law Union	17th Century Landowner
Gresteel More	Faughanvale	Faughanvale	Ballykelly	Limavady	Fishmongers
Grillagh	Maghera	Maghera	Maghera	Magherafelt	Vintners
Gulladuff	Gulladuff	Maghera	Maghera	Magherafelt	Vintners
Halfgayne	Tullykeeran	Killelagh	Maghera	Magherafelt	Vintners
Harpurs Hill	Knockantern	Coleraine	Coleraine	Coleraine	Irish Society
Hass	Dungiven	Dungiven	Dungiven	Limavady	Skinners
Heagles	Knockantern	Ballymoney	Coleraine	Coleraine	Earl of Antrim
Highmoor	Tamnaherin	Cumber Lower	Eglinton	Londonderry	Grocers
Hunter's Glebe	Downhill	Dunboe	Articlave	Coleraine	Churchland
Inchadoghill	Agivey	Aghadowey	Aghadowey	Coleraine	Ironmongers
Inchmearing	Ballylagan	Ballywillin	Portstewart	Coleraine	Irish Society
Iniscarn	Iniscarn	Desertmartin	Draperstown	Magherafelt	Drapers
Inisconagher	Gelvin	Bovevagh	Dungiven	Limavady	Churchland
Inishrush	Clady	Tamlaght O'Crilly	Bellaghy	Magherafelt	Vintners
Inshaleen	Garvagh	Errigal	Garvagh	Coleraine	Ironmongers
Intake Lough Beg	Bellaghy	Ballyscullion	Bellaghy	Magherafelt	Churchland
Intake Lough Beg	Castle Dawson	Ballyscullion	Bellaghy	Magherafelt	Salters
Island Effrick North	Knockantern	Ballyrashane	Coleraine	Coleraine	Irish Society
Island Effrick South	Knockantern	Ballyrashane	Coleraine	Coleraine	Irish Society
Island Flackey	Ballylagan	Ballywillin	Portstewart	Coleraine	Irish Society
Island Heaghey	Knockantern	Coleraine	Coleraine	Coleraine	Irish Society
Island Tasserty	Portstewart	Ballyaghran	Portstewart	Coleraine	Irish Society
Island Vardin	Portstewart	Ballyaghran	Portstewart	Coleraine	Irish Society
Islandmore Lower	Ballylagan	Ballywillin	Portstewart	Coleraine	Irish Society
Islandmore Upper	Ballylagan	Ballywillin	Portstewart	Coleraine	Irish Society
Keady	Keady	Drumachose	Limavady	Limavady	Merchant Taylors
Keady	Swatragh	Maghera	Maghera	Magherafelt	Mercers
Keely	Aghadowey	Aghadowey	Aghadowey	Coleraine	Churchland
Keenaght	Iniscarn	Kilcronaghan	Draperstown	Magherafelt	Drapers
Kilcaltan	Bondsglen	Cumber Upper	Claudy	Londonderry	Skinners
Kilcreen	Banagher	Learmount	Claudy	Londonderry	Skinners
Kilculmagrandal	Foreglen	Cumber Upper	Feeny	Limavady	Fishmongers
Kildoag	Bondsglen	Cumber Lower	Claudy	Londonderry	Skinners
Kilfinnan	Waterside	Clondermot	Waterside Rural	Londonderry	Churchland
Kilgort	Ballymullins	Learmount	Claudy	Londonderry	Fishmongers
Kilhoyle	Lislane	Balteagh	Limavady	Limavady	Haberdashers
Killaloo	Bondsglen	Cumber Lower	Claudy	Londonderry	Skinners
Killane (part of)	Fruithill	Drumachose	Limavady	Limavady	Phillips
Killcranny	Bannbrook	Killowen	Articlave	Coleraine	Clothworkers
Killea	Liberties Upper	Templemore	Liberties Upper	Londonderry	Irish Society
Killeague	Drumcroon	Aghadowey	Aghadowey	Coleraine	Ironmongers

Townland	D.E.D.	Parish	Registrar District	Poor Law Union	17th Century Landowner
Killennan	Tamnaherin	Cumber Lower	Eglinton	Londonderry	Goldsmiths
Killibleught	Straw	Bovevagh	Ballykelly	Limavady	Churchland
Killunaght	Owenreagh	Banagher	Feeny	Limavady	Churchland
Killure	Drumcroon	Macosquin	Aghadowey	Coleraine	Ironmongers
Killybasky	Lissan Upper	Lissan	Moneymore	Magherafelt	Churchland
Killybearn	Moneyhaw	Derryloran	Moneymore	Magherafelt	Drapers
Killyberry	Bellaghy	Ballyscullion	Bellaghy	Magherafelt	Phillips
Killyberry Boyd	Bellaghy	Ballyscullion	Bellaghy	Magherafelt	Phillips
Killyberry Downing	Bellaghy	Ballyscullion	Bellaghy	Magherafelt	Phillips
Killyboggin	Ballymoghan	Desertmartin	Magherafelt	Magherafelt	Salters
Killybready	Aghanloo	Aghanloo	Bellarena	Limavady	Haberdashers
Killycor	Foreglen	Cumber Upper	Feeny	Limavady	Fishmongers
Killyfaddy	Ballymoghan	Magherafelt	Magherafelt	Magherafelt	Salters
Killygreen Lower	Ballylagan	Ballywillin	Portstewart	Coleraine	Irish Society
Killygreen Upper	Ballylagan	Ballywillin	Portstewart	Coleraine	Irish Society
Killygullib Glebe	Hervey Hill	Tamlaght O'Crilly	Kilrea	Coleraine	Churchland
Killykergan	Aghadowey	Aghadowey	Aghadowey	Coleraine	Churchland
Killylane	Faughanvale	Faughanvale	Ballykelly	Limavady	Fishmongers
Killymallaght	Glendermot	Clondermot	Waterside Rural	Londonderry	Goldsmiths
Killymuck	Salterstown	Ballinderry	Magherafelt	Magherafelt	Churchland
Killymuck Glebe	Tamlaght	Tamlaght O'Crilly	Kilrea	Coleraine	Churchland
Killyneese	Magherafelt	Magherafelt	Magherafelt	Magherafelt	Salters
Killynumber	Iniscarn	Kilcronaghan	Draperstown	Magherafelt	Drapers
Killytoney	Iniscarn	Kilcronaghan	Draperstown	Magherafelt	Drapers
Killyvally	Garvagh	Desertoghill	Garvagh	Coleraine	Churchland
Killyveety	Articlave	Dunboe	Articlave	Coleraine	Clothworkers
Killywool	Faughanvale	Faughanvale	Ballykelly	Limavady	Churchland
Kilmaconnell	Somerset	Macosquin	Aghadowey	Coleraine	Merchant Taylors
Kilnappy	Lough Enagh	Faughanvale	Eglinton	Londonderry	Grocers
Kilrea	Kilrea	Kilrea	Kilrea	Coleraine	Mercers
Kilrea, Bridge Street	Kilrea	Kilrea	Kilrea	Coleraine	Mercers
Kilrea, Church Street	Kilrea	Kilrea	Kilrea	Coleraine	Mercers
Kilrea, Coleraine Street	Kilrea	Kilrea	Kilrea	Coleraine	Mercers
Kilrea, Diamond	Kilrea	Kilrea	Kilrea	Coleraine	Mercers
Kilrea, Maghera Street	Kilrea	Kilrea	Kilrea	Coleraine	Mercers
Kiltest	Ringsend	Aghadowey	Aghadowey	Coleraine	Merchant Taylors
Kiltinny Beg	Portstewart	Ballyaghran	Portstewart	Coleraine	Irish Society
Kiltinny Lower	Letterloan	Macosquin	Articlave	Coleraine	Merchant Taylors

Townland	D.E.D.	Parish	Registrar District	Poor Law Union	17th Century Landowner
Kiltinny More	Portstewart	Ballyaghran	Portstewart	Coleraine	Irish Society
Kiltinny Upper	Letterloan	Macosquin	Articlave	Coleraine	Merchant Taylors
Kinculbrack	Foreglen	Cumber Upper	Feeny	Limavady	Fishmongers
Kinnyglass	Drumcroon	Macosquin	Aghadowey	Coleraine	Ironmongers
Kirkistown	Knockantern	Ballyrashane	Coleraine	Coleraine	Irish Society
Kirley	Carnamoney	Maghera	Draperstown	Magherafelt	Drapers
Kittybane	Glendermot	Clondermot	Waterside Rural	Londonderry	Goldsmiths
Knockadoo	Lissan Upper	Lissan	Moneymore	Magherafelt	Churchland
Knockaduff	Agivey	Aghadowey	Aghadowey	Coleraine	Ironmongers
Knockan	Feeny	Banagher	Feeny	Limavady	Churchland
Knockantern	Knockantern	Coleraine	Coleraine	Coleraine	Irish Society
Knockbrack	Ardmore	Clondermot	Waterside Rural	Londonderry	Grocers
Knockmult	Articlave	Formoyle	Articlave	Coleraine	Clothworkers
Knocknagin	Desertmartin	Desertmartin	Magherafelt	Magherafelt	Churchland
Knocknakeeragh	Knockantern	Ballyrashane	Coleraine	Coleraine	Irish Society
Knocknakielt	Maghera	Termoneeny	Maghera	Magherafelt	Churchland
Knocknogher	Articlave	Dunboe	Articlave	Coleraine	Clothworkers
Knockoneill	Swatragh	Killelagh	Maghera	Magherafelt	Mercers
Kurin	Garvagh	Desertoghill	Garvagh	Coleraine	Churchland
Labby	Bancran	Ballynascreen	Draperstown	Magherafelt	Skinners
Lackagh	Bondsglen	Cumber Lower	Claudy	Londonderry	Skinners
Lackagh	Dungiven	Dungiven	Dungiven	Limavady	Skinners
Landagivey	Agivey	Agivey	Aghadowey	Coleraine	Ironmongers
Landmore	Agivey	Aghadowey	Aghadowey	Coleraine	Ironmongers
Laragh	The Grove	Desertoghill	Kilrea	Coleraine	Mercers
Laraghaleas	Eglinton	Faughanvale	Eglinton	Londonderry	Grocers
Largantea	Aghanloo	Aghanloo	Bellarena	Limavady	Haberdashers
Largantogher	Maghera	Maghera	Maghera	Magherafelt	Churchland
Largy	The Highlands	Carrick	Ballykelly	Limavady	Phillips
Largyreagh	Keady	Drumachose	Limavady	Limavady	Haberdashers
Larrycormick	Moneymore	Desertlyn	Moneymore	Magherafelt	Drapers
Lear	Ballymullins	Learmount	Claudy	Londonderry	Skinners
Learden	Drumcroon	Macosquin	Aghadowey	Coleraine	Merchant Taylors
Leck	Keady	Drumachose	Limavady	Limavady	Haberdashers
Leck	Letterloan	Macosquin	Articlave	Coleraine	Merchant Taylors
Leckagh	Magherafelt	Magherafelt	Magherafelt	Magherafelt	Salters
Lecumpher	Brackagh Slieve Gallion	Desertmartin	Moneymore	Magherafelt	Drapers
Leeke	Straw	Bovevagh	Ballykelly	Limavady	Phillips
Legaghory	Bondsglen	Cumber Lower	Claudy	Londonderry	Skinners
Legavannon	Faughanvale	Faughanvale	Ballykelly	Limavady	Churchland
Leitrim	Castle Dawson	Ballyscullion	Bellaghy	Magherafelt	Phillips

Townland	D.E.D.	Parish	Registrar District	Poor Law Union	17th Century Landowner
Lemnaroy	Rocktown	Termoneeny	Bellaghy	Magherafelt	Vintners
Lenamore	Gelvin	Dungiven	Dungiven	Limavady	Haberdashers
Lenamore	Bellarena	Magilligan	Bellarena	Limavady	Churchland
Letteran	Lissan Upper	Lissan	Moneymore	Magherafelt	Churchland
Letterloan	Letterloan	Macosquin	Articlave	Coleraine	Merchant Taylors
Letterlogher	Foreglen	Cumber Upper	Feeny	Limavady	Fishmongers
Lettermire	Bondsglen	Cumber Lower	Claudy	Londonderry	Skinners
Lettermuck	Claudy	Cumber Upper	Claudy	Londonderry	Skinners
Lettershendony	Tamnaherin	Cumber Lower	Eglinton	Londonderry	Grocers
Liffock	Articlave	Dunboe	Articlave	Coleraine	Clothworkers
Ligg	Lough Enagh	Faughanvale	Eglinton	Londonderry	Grocers
Limavady, Ballyclose Street	Limavady	Drumachose	Limavady	Limavady	Phillips
Limavady, Billy's Street	Limavady	Drumachose	Limavady	Limavady	Phillips
Limavady, Catherine Street	Limavady	Drumachose	Limavady	Limavady	Phillips
Limavady, Distillery Road	Limavady	Drumachose	Limavady	Limavady	Phillips
Limavady, Flemings Court	Limavady	Drumachose	Limavady	Limavady	Phillips
Limavady, Irish Green Street	Limavady	Drumachose	Limavady	Limavady	Phillips
Limavady, Irish Green Street	Limavady	Drumachose	Limavady	Limavady	Phillips
Limavady, Isle of Man Street	Limavady	Drumachose	Limavady	Limavady	Phillips
Limavady, Kennaught Street	Limavady	Drumachose	Limavady	Limavady	Phillips
Limavady, Linenhall Street	Limavady	Drumachose	Limavady	Limavady	Phillips
Limavady, Main Street	Limavady	Drumachose	Limavady	Limavady	Phillips
Limavady, Market House Street	Limavady	Drumachose	Limavady	Limavady	Phillips
Limavady, Meeting House Street	Limavady	Drumachose	Limavady	Limavady	Phillips
Limavady, Methodist Lane	Limavady	Drumachose	Limavady	Limavady	Phillips
Limavady, Mill Row	Limavady	Drumachose	Limavady	Limavady	Phillips
Limavady, Protestant Street	Limavady	Drumachose	Limavady	Limavady	Phillips
Limavady, Roe Mill Street	Limavady	Drumachose	Limavady	Limavady	Phillips
Limavady, Sandy Row	Limavady	Drumachose	Limavady	Limavady	Phillips
Limavady, Steels Row	Limavady	Drumachose	Limavady	Limavady	Phillips
Limavady, William Street	Limavady	Drumachose	Limavady	Limavady	Phillips

Townland	D.E.D.	Parish	Registrar District	Poor Law Union	17th Century Landowner
Ling	Ballymullins	Cumber Upper	Claudy	Londonderry	Skinners
Lisachrin	The Grove	Desertoghill	Kilrea	Coleraine	Mercers
Lisaghmore or The Trench	Waterside	Clondermot	Waterside Rural	Londonderry	Goldsmiths
Lisalbanagh	Brackagh Slieve Gallion	Desertlyn	Moneymore	Magherafelt	Drapers
Lisboy	Aghadowey	Aghadowey	Aghadowey	Coleraine	Churchland
Lisbunny	Ballymullins	Cumber Upper	Claudy	Londonderry	Skinners
Liscall	Glenkeen	Errigal	Garvagh	Coleraine	Ironmongers
Lisdillon	Ardmore	Clondermot	Waterside Rural	Londonderry	Grocers
Lisglass	Glendermot	Clondermot	Waterside Rural	Londonderry	Grocers
Lisgorgan Glebe	Tamlaght	Tamlaght O'Crilly	Kilrea	Coleraine	Churchland
Lislane	Lislane	Balteagh	Limavady	Limavady	Haberdashers
Lislea	Tamlaght	Kilrea	Kilrea	Coleraine	Mercers
Lismacarol	Waterside	Clondermot	Waterside Rural	Londonderry	Goldsmiths
Lismoney	Moneyhaw	Lissan	Moneymore	Magherafelt	Drapers
Lismoyle	The Grove	Tamlaght O'Crilly	Kilrea	Coleraine	Mercers
Lismurphy	Somerset	Macosquin	Aghadowey	Coleraine	Merchant Taylors
Lisnagalt	Knockantern	Ballyrashane	Coleraine	Coleraine	Irish Society
Lisnagelvin	Waterside	Clondermot	Waterside Rural	Londonderry	Churchland
Lisnagrib	Aghanloo	Aghanloo	Bellarena	Limavady	Haberdashers
Lisnagroat	Tamlaght	Tamlaght O'Crilly	Kilrea	Coleraine	Mercers
Lisnakilly	Fruithill	Tamlaght Finlagan	Limavady	Limavady	Fishmongers
Lisnamorrow	Ballyronan	Artrea	Magherafelt	Magherafelt	Salters
Lisnamuck	Aghadowey	Aghadowey	Aghadowey	Coleraine	Churchland
Lisnamuck	Carnamoney	Maghera	Draperstown	Magherafelt	Drapers
Lisnascreghog	Slaght	Errigal	Garvagh	Coleraine	Ironmongers
Lisneal	Waterside	Clondermot	Waterside Rural	Londonderry	Churchland
Lissaghmore	Agivey	Agivey	Aghadowey	Coleraine	Ironmongers
Lissahawley	Lough Enagh	Clondermot	Eglinton	Londonderry	Churchland
Lissan Demesne	Lissan Upper	Lissan	Moneymore	Magherafelt	Churchland
Listress	Tamnaherin	Cumber Lower	Eglinton	Londonderry	Grocers
Liswatty Lower	Knockantern	Ballyrashane	Coleraine	Coleraine	Irish Society
Liswatty Upper	Knockantern	Ballyrashane	Coleraine	Coleraine	Irish Society
Little Derry	Lislane	Balteagh	Limavady	Limavady	Haberdashers
Little Glebe	Downhill	Dunboe	Articlave	Coleraine	Churchland
Lodge	Knockantern	Coleraine	Coleraine	Coleraine	Irish Society
Loguestown	Ballylagan	Ballywillin	Portstewart	Coleraine	Irish Society
Loguestown	Ballylagan	Coleraine	Portstewart	Coleraine	Irish Society
Lomond	Myroe	Tamlaght Finlagan	Bellarena	Limavady	Phillips

Townland	D.E.D.	Parish	Registrar District	Poor Law Union	17th Century Landowner
Londonderry, Abbey Street	Londonderry Urban No. 4	Templemore	Londonderry Urban No. 2	Londonderry	Irish Society
Londonderry, Abercorn Place	Londonderry Urban No. 3	Templemore	Londonderry Urban No. 1	Londonderry	Irish Society
Londonderry, Abercorn Quay	Londonderry Urban No. 3	Templemore	Londonderry Urban No. 1	Londonderry	Irish Society
Londonderry, Abercorn Road	Londonderry Urban No. 2	Templemore	Londonderry Urban No. 1	Londonderry	Irish Society
Londonderry, Abercorn Road	Londonderry Urban No. 3	Templemore	Londonderry Urban No. 1	Londonderry	Irish Society
Londonderry, Academy Road	Londonderry Urban No. 1	Templemore	Londonderry Urban No. 2	Londonderry	Irish Society
Londonderry, Academy Road	Londonderry Urban No. 1	Templemore	Londonderry Urban No. 2	Londonderry	Irish Society
Londonderry, Adair Street	Londonderry Urban No. 2	Templemore	Londonderry Urban No. 1	Londonderry	Irish Society
Londonderry, Adam Street	Londonderry Urban No. 4	Templemore	Londonderry Urban No. 2	Londonderry	Irish Society
Londonderry, Albert Place	Londonderry Urban No. 3	Templemore	Londonderry Urban No. 1	Londonderry	Irish Society
Londonderry, Albert Street	Londonderry Urban No. 3	Templemore	Londonderry Urban No. 1	Londonderry	Irish Society
Londonderry, Alexander Place	Waterside	Clondermot	Waterside Urban	Londonderry	Irish Society
Londonderry, Alexander Place	Londonderry Urban No. 2	Templemore	Londonderry Urban No. 1	Londonderry	Irish Society
Londonderry, Alma Place	Londonderry Urban No. 2	Templemore	Londonderry Urban No. 1	Londonderry	Irish Society
Londonderry, Ann Street	Londonderry Urban No. 4	Templemore	Londonderry Urban No. 2	Londonderry	Irish Society
Londonderry, Anne Street	Londonderry Urban No. 2	Templemore	Londonderry Urban No. 1	Londonderry	Irish Society
Londonderry, Argyle Street	Londonderry Urban No. 1	Templemore	Londonderry Urban No. 2	Londonderry	Irish Society
Londonderry, Argyle Terrace	Londonderry Urban No. 1	Templemore	Londonderry Urban No. 2	Londonderry	Irish Society
Londonderry, Artillery Street	Londonderry Urban No. 3	Templemore	Londonderry Urban No. 1	Londonderry	Irish Society
Londonderry, Artisan Street	Londonderry Urban No. 1	Templemore	Londonderry Urban No. 2	Londonderry	Irish Society
Londonderry, Ashcroft Place	Waterside	Clondermot	Waterside Urban	Londonderry	Irish Society
Londonderry, Asylum Road	Londonderry Urban No. 1	Templemore	Londonderry Urban No. 2	Londonderry	Irish Society
Londonderry, Aubrey Street	Londonderry Urban No. 3	Templemore	Londonderry Urban No. 1	Londonderry	Irish Society
Londonderry, Bank Place	Londonderry Urban No. 3	Templemore	Londonderry Urban No. 1	Londonderry	Irish Society
Londonderry, Barnewall Place	Waterside	Clondermot	Waterside Urban	Londonderry	Irish Society
Londonderry, Barrack Street	Londonderry Urban No. 2	Templemore	Londonderry Urban No. 2	Londonderry	Irish Society
Londonderry, Barry Street	Londonderry Urban No. 1	Templemore	Londonderry Urban No. 2	Londonderry	Irish Society
Londonderry, Beechwood Avenue	Londonderry Urban No. 1	Templemore	Londonderry Urban No. 2	Londonderry	Irish Society

Townland	D.E.D.	Parish	Registrar District	Poor Law Union	17th Century Landowner
Londonderry, Bellview	Waterside	Clondermot	Waterside Urban	Londonderry	Irish Society
Londonderry, Bennett Street	Londonderry Urban No. 2	Templemore	Londonderry Urban No. 1	Londonderry	Irish Society
Londonderry, Bennett Street	Londonderry Urban No. 3	Templemore	Londonderry Urban No. 1	Londonderry	Irish Society
Londonderry, Bentley Street	Waterside	Clondermot	Waterside Urban	Londonderry	Irish Society
Londonderry, Benvarden Avenue	Waterside	Clondermot	Waterside Urban	Londonderry	Irish Society
Londonderry, Bishop Street	Londonderry Urban No. 2	Templemore	Londonderry Urban No. 1	Londonderry	Irish Society
Londonderry, Bishop Street	Londonderry Urban No. 3	Templemore	Londonderry Urban No. 1	Londonderry	Irish Society
Londonderry, Bishop Street	Londonderry Urban No. 3	Templemore	Londonderry Urban No. 1	Londonderry	Irish Society
Londonderry, Bishop Street	Londonderry Urban No. 4	Templemore	Londonderry Urban No. 2	Londonderry	Irish Society
Londonderry, Bishop Street	Londonderry Urban No. 4	Templemore	Londonderry Urban No. 2	Londonderry	Irish Society
Londonderry, Bishop Street	Londonderry Urban No. 2	Templemore	Londonderry Urban No. 1	Londonderry	Irish Society
Londonderry, Blucher Street	Londonderry Urban No. 4	Templemore	Londonderry Urban No. 2	Londonderry	Irish Society
Londonderry, Bond's Field	Waterside	Clondermot	Waterside Urban	Londonderry	Irish Society
Londonderry, Bond's Hill	Waterside	Clondermot	Waterside Urban	Londonderry	Irish Society
Londonderry, Bond's Place	Waterside	Clondermot	Waterside Urban	Londonderry	Irish Society
Londonderry, Bond's Street	Waterside	Clondermot	Waterside Urban	Londonderry	Irish Society
Londonderry, Brandywell Road	Londonderry Urban No. 2	Templemore	Londonderry Urban No. 2	Londonderry	Irish Society
Londonderry, Bridge Street	Londonderry Urban No. 3	Templemore	Londonderry Urban No. 1	Londonderry	Irish Society
Londonderry, Brook Street Avenue	Londonderry Urban No. 2	Templemore	Londonderry Urban No. 1	Londonderry	Irish Society
Londonderry, Butcher Street	Londonderry Urban No. 4	Templemore	Londonderry Urban No. 2	Londonderry	Irish Society
Londonderry, Cable Street	Londonderry Urban No. 4	Templemore	Londonderry Urban No. 2	Londonderry	Irish Society
Londonderry, Carlin Street	Waterside	Clondermot	Waterside Urban	Londonderry	Irish Society
Londonderry, Carlisle Pass	Londonderry Urban No. 3	Templemore	Londonderry Urban No. 1	Londonderry	Irish Society
Londonderry, Carlisle Road	Londonderry Urban No. 3	Templemore	Londonderry Urban No. 1	Londonderry	Irish Society
Londonderry, Caroline Place	Londonderry Urban No. 4	Templemore	Londonderry Urban No. 2	Londonderry	Irish Society
Londonderry, Carrigans Lane	Londonderry Urban No. 2	Templemore	Londonderry Urban No. 1	Londonderry	Irish Society
Londonderry, Castle Street	Londonderry Urban No. 1	Templemore	Londonderry Urban No. 2	Londonderry	Irish Society
Londonderry, Castle Street	Londonderry Urban No. 4	Templemore	Londonderry Urban No. 2	Londonderry	Irish Society

Townland	D.E.D.	Parish	Registrar District	Poor Law Union	17th Century Landowner
Londonderry, Cedar Street	Londonderry Urban No. 1	Templemore	Londonderry Urban No. 2	Londonderry	Irish Society
Londonderry, Chamberlain Street	Londonderry Urban No. 1	Templemore	Londonderry Urban No. 2	Londonderry	Irish Society
Londonderry, Chamberlain Street	Londonderry Urban No. 4	Templemore	Londonderry Urban No. 2	Londonderry	Irish Society
Londonderry, Chapel Road	Waterside	Clondermot	Waterside Urban	Londonderry	Irish Society
Londonderry, Charlotte Place	Londonderry Urban No. 2	Templemore	Londonderry Urban No. 2	Londonderry	Irish Society
Londonderry, Charlotte Street	Londonderry Urban No. 2	Templemore	Londonderry Urban No. 2	Londonderry	Irish Society
Londonderry, Church Wall	Londonderry Urban No. 3	Templemore	Londonderry Urban No. 1	Londonderry	Irish Society
Londonderry, Clarence Avenue	Londonderry Urban No. 1	Templemore	Londonderry Urban No. 2	Londonderry	Irish Society
Londonderry, Clarence Place	Londonderry Urban No. 3	Templemore	Londonderry Urban No. 1	Londonderry	Irish Society
Londonderry, Clarendon Street	Londonderry Urban No. 1	Templemore	Londonderry Urban No. 2	Londonderry	Irish Society
Londonderry, Clarendon Street Lower	Londonderry Urban No. 1	Templemore	Londonderry Urban No. 2	Londonderry	Irish Society
Londonderry, Clooney Road	Waterside	Clondermot	Waterside Urban	Londonderry	Irish Society
Londonderry, Clooney Terrace	Waterside	Clondermot	Waterside Urban	Londonderry	Irish Society
Londonderry, Clyde Street	Londonderry Urban No. 1	Templemore	Londonderry Urban No. 2	Londonderry	Irish Society
Londonderry, Cochrane's Row	Waterside	Clondermot	Waterside Urban	Londonderry	Irish Society
Londonderry, College Avenue	Londonderry Urban No. 1	Templemore	Londonderry Urban No. 2	Londonderry	Irish Society
Londonderry, College Terrace	Londonderry Urban No. 1	Templemore	Londonderry Urban No. 2	Londonderry	Irish Society
Londonderry, Columba Terrace	Waterside	Clondermot	Waterside Urban	Londonderry	Irish Society
Londonderry, Cottage Row	Londonderry Urban No. 1	Templemore	Londonderry Urban No. 2	Londonderry	Irish Society
Londonderry, Crawford Square	Londonderry Urban No. 1	Templemore	Londonderry Urban No. 2	Londonderry	Irish Society
Londonderry, Creggan Road	Londonderry Urban No. 1	Templemore	Londonderry Urban No. 2	Londonderry	Irish Society
Londonderry, Creggan Street	Londonderry Urban No. 1	Templemore	Londonderry Urban No. 2	Londonderry	Irish Society
Londonderry, Creggan Street	Londonderry Urban No. 4	Templemore	Londonderry Urban No. 2	Londonderry	Irish Society
Londonderry, Creggan Terrace	Londonderry Urban No. 4	Templemore	Londonderry Urban No. 2	Londonderry	Irish Society
Londonderry, Cross Street	Waterside	Clondermot	Waterside Urban	Londonderry	Irish Society
Londonderry, Cross Street	Londonderry Urban No. 1	Templemore	Londonderry Urban No. 2	Londonderry	Irish Society
Londonderry, Cunningham Row	Londonderry Urban No. 4	Templemore	Londonderry Urban No. 2	Londonderry	Irish Society

Townland	D.E.D.	Parish	Registrar District	Poor Law Union	17th Century Landowner
Londonderry, Custom House Street	Londonderry Urban No. 1	Templemore	Londonderry Urban No. 2	Londonderry	Irish Society
Londonderry, Cuthbert Street	Waterside	Clondermot	Waterside Urban	Londonderry	Irish Society
Londonderry, Dark Lane	Londonderry Urban No. 2	Templemore	Londonderry Urban No. 2	Londonderry	Irish Society
Londonderry, De Burgh Square	Londonderry Urban No. 1	Templemore	Londonderry Urban No. 2	Londonderry	Irish Society
Londonderry, De Burgh Terrace	Londonderry Urban No. 1	Templemore	Londonderry Urban No. 2	Londonderry	Irish Society
Londonderry, Deanery Street	Londonderry Urban No. 2	Templemore	Londonderry Urban No. 2	Londonderry	Irish Society
Londonderry, Derry View	Waterside	Clondermot	Waterside Urban	Londonderry	Irish Society
Londonderry, Derryview Terrace	Waterside	Clondermot	Waterside Urban	Londonderry	Irish Society
Londonderry, Dervock Place	Waterside	Clondermot	Waterside Urban	Londonderry	Irish Society
Londonderry, Diamond	Londonderry Urban No. 3	Templemore	Londonderry Urban No. 1	Londonderry	Irish Society
Diamond	Urban No. 4		Urban No. 2		
Londonderry, Dickson's Close	Londonderry Urban No. 1	Templemore	Londonderry Urban No. 2	Londonderry	Irish Society
Londonderry, Distillery Brae	Waterside	Clondermot	Waterside Urban	Londonderry	Irish Society
Londonderry, Distillery Lane	Waterside	Clondermot	Waterside Urban	Londonderry	Irish Society
Londonderry, Dock Terrace	Londonderry Urban No. 3	Templemore	Londonderry Urban No. 1	Londonderry	Irish Society
Londonderry, Donaghy's Close	Londonderry Urban No. 2	Templemore	Londonderry Urban No. 2	Londonderry	Irish Society
Londonderry, Donegal Place	Londonderry Urban No. 2	Templemore	Londonderry Urban No. 2	Londonderry	Irish Society
Londonderry, Donegal Street	Londonderry Urban No. 1	Templemore	Londonderry Urban No. 2	Londonderry	Irish Society
Londonderry, Duddy's Row	Waterside	Clondermot	Waterside Urban	Londonderry	Irish Society
Londonderry, Duke Street	Waterside	Clondermot	Waterside Urban	Londonderry	Irish Society
Londonderry, Duncreggan Road	Londonderry Urban No. 1	Templemore	Londonderry Urban No. 2	Londonderry	Irish Society
Londonderry, Dunfield Terrace	Waterside	Clondermot	Waterside Urban	Londonderry	Irish Society
Londonderry, Dungiven Road	Waterside	Clondermot	Waterside Urban	Londonderry	Irish Society
Londonderry, Dungiven Road Close	Waterside	Clondermot	Waterside Urban	Londonderry	Irish Society
Londonderry, East Wall	Londonderry Urban No. 3	Templemore	Londonderry Urban No. 1	Londonderry	Irish Society
Londonderry, Ebrington Barracks	Waterside	Clondermot	Waterside Urban	Londonderry	Irish Society
Londonderry, Ebrington Gardens	Waterside	Clondermot	Waterside Urban	Londonderry	Irish Society

Townland	D.E.D.	Parish	Registrar District	Poor Law Union	17th Century Landowner
Londonderry, Ebrington Terrace	Waterside	Clondermot	Waterside Urban	Londonderry	Irish Society
Londonderry, Eden Place	Londonderry Urban No. 4	Templemore	Londonderry Urban No. 2	Londonderry	Irish Society
Londonderry, Edenmore Street	Londonderry Urban No. 1	Templemore	Londonderry Urban No. 2	Londonderry	Irish Society
Londonderry, Edward Street	Londonderry Urban No. 1	Templemore	Londonderry Urban No. 2	Londonderry	Irish Society
Londonderry, Eglinton Place	Londonderry Urban No. 4	Templemore	Londonderry Urban No. 2	Londonderry	Irish Society
Londonderry, Elmwood Street	Londonderry Urban No. 4	Templemore	Londonderry Urban No. 2	Londonderry	Irish Society
Londonderry, Emerson Street	Waterside	Clondermot	Waterside Urban	Londonderry	Irish Society
Londonderry, Epworth Street	Londonderry Urban No. 1	Templemore	Londonderry Urban No. 2	Londonderry	Irish Society
Londonderry, Ewing Street	Londonderry Urban No. 2	Templemore	Londonderry Urban No. 2	Londonderry	Irish Society
Londonderry, Fahan Street	Londonderry Urban No. 4	Templemore	Londonderry Urban No. 2	Londonderry	Irish Society
Londonderry, Fahan Street	Londonderry Urban No. 4	Templemore	Londonderry Urban No. 2	Londonderry	Irish Society
Londonderry, Ferguson Street	Londonderry Urban No. 2	Templemore	Londonderry Urban No. 1	Londonderry	Irish Society
Londonderry, Ferryquay Street	Londonderry Urban No. 3	Templemore	Londonderry Urban No. 1	Londonderry	Irish Society
Londonderry, Florence Street	Londonderry Urban No. 1	Templemore	Londonderry Urban No. 2	Londonderry	Irish Society
Londonderry, Fountain Hill	Waterside	Clondermot	Waterside Urban	Londonderry	Irish Society
Londonderry, Fountain Place	Londonderry Urban No. 3	Templemore	Londonderry Urban No. 1	Londonderry	Irish Society
Londonderry, Fountain Street	Londonderry Urban No. 3	Templemore	Londonderry Urban No. 1	Londonderry	Irish Society
Londonderry, Fountain Street	Londonderry Urban No. 3	Templemore	Londonderry Urban No. 1	Londonderry	Irish Society
Londonderry, Fox's Lane	Londonderry Urban No. 1	Templemore	Londonderry Urban No. 2	Londonderry	Irish Society
Londonderry, Foyle Road	Londonderry Urban No. 2	Templemore	Londonderry Urban No. 1	Londonderry	Irish Society
Londonderry, Foyle Road	Londonderry Urban No. 3	Templemore	Londonderry Urban No. 1	Londonderry	Irish Society
Londonderry, Foyle Street	Londonderry Urban No. 3	Templemore	Londonderry Urban No. 1	Londonderry	Irish Society
Londonderry, Foyle View	Londonderry Urban No. 2	Templemore	Londonderry Urban No. 1	Londonderry	Irish Society
Londonderry, Frances Street	Londonderry Urban No. 1	Templemore	Londonderry Urban No. 2	Londonderry	Irish Society
Londonderry, Frederick Street	Londonderry Urban No. 4	Templemore	Londonderry Urban No. 2	Londonderry	Irish Society
Londonderry, Fulton Place	Londonderry Urban No. 2	Templemore	Londonderry Urban No. 2	Londonderry	Irish Society
Londonderry, Gallagher's Square	Londonderry Urban No. 4	Templemore	Londonderry Urban No. 2	Londonderry	Irish Society
Londonderry, George Street	Londonderry Urban No. 3	Templemore	Londonderry Urban No. 1	Londonderry	Irish Society

Townland	D.E.D.	Parish	Registrar District	Poor Law Union	17th Century Landowner
Londonderry, Glasgow Street	Londonderry Urban No. 1	Templemore	Londonderry Urban No. 2	Londonderry	Irish Society
Londonderry, Glasgow Terrace	Londonderry Urban No. 1	Templemore	Londonderry Urban No. 2	Londonderry	Irish Society
Londonderry, Glen Road	Londonderry Urban No. 1	Templemore	Londonderry Urban No. 2	Londonderry	Irish Society
Londonderry, Glenbrook Terrace	Londonderry Urban No. 1	Templemore	Londonderry Urban No. 2	Londonderry	Irish Society
Londonderry, Glendermott Road	Waterside	Clondermot	Waterside Urban	Londonderry	Irish Society
Londonderry, Gordon Place	Londonderry Urban No. 2	Templemore	Londonderry Urban No. 2	Londonderry	Irish Society
Londonderry, Gordon Terrace	Londonderry Urban No. 2	Templemore	Londonderry Urban No. 2	Londonderry	Irish Society
Londonderry, Gortfoyle Place	Waterside	Clondermot	Waterside Urban	Londonderry	Irish Society
Londonderry, Governor Road	Londonderry Urban No. 1	Templemore	Londonderry Urban No. 2	Londonderry	Irish Society
Londonderry, Grafton Street	Londonderry Urban No. 1	Templemore	Londonderry Urban No. 2	Londonderry	Irish Society
Londonderry, Great James Street	Londonderry Urban No. 1	Templemore	Londonderry Urban No. 2	Londonderry	Irish Society
Londonderry, Gresham's Close	Londonderry Urban No. 2	Templemore	Londonderry Urban No. 2	Londonderry	Irish Society
Londonderry, Grove Place	Londonderry Urban No. 3	Templemore	Londonderry Urban No. 1	Londonderry	Irish Society
Londonderry, Guildhall Street	Londonderry Urban No. 1	Templemore	Londonderry Urban No. 2	Londonderry	Irish Society
Londonderry, Hamilton Street	Londonderry Urban No. 2	Templemore	Londonderry Urban No. 2	Londonderry	Irish Society
Londonderry, Harding Street	Londonderry Urban No. 3	Templemore	Londonderry Urban No. 1	Londonderry	Irish Society
Londonderry, Harvey Street	Londonderry Urban No. 1	Templemore	Londonderry Urban No. 2	Londonderry	Irish Society
Londonderry, Harvey Street	Londonderry Urban No. 4	Templemore	Londonderry Urban No. 2	Londonderry	Irish Society
Londonderry, Hawkins Street	Londonderry Urban No. 3	Templemore	Londonderry Urban No. 1	Londonderry	Irish Society
Londonderry, Hawthorn Terrace	Londonderry Urban No. 1	Templemore	Londonderry Urban No. 2	Londonderry	Irish Society
Londonderry, Henrietta Street	Londonderry Urban No. 2	Templemore	Londonderry Urban No. 2	Londonderry	Irish Society
Londonderry, Henry Street	Londonderry Urban No. 3	Templemore	Londonderry Urban No. 1	Londonderry	Irish Society
Londonderry, High Street	Londonderry Urban No. 1	Templemore	Londonderry Urban No. 2	Londonderry	Irish Society
Londonderry, Hogg's Folly	Londonderry Urban No. 2	Templemore	Londonderry Urban No. 2	Londonderry	Irish Society
Londonderry, Hollywell Street	Londonderry Urban No. 2	Templemore	Londonderry Urban No. 2	Londonderry	Irish Society
Londonderry, Horace Street	Londonderry Urban No. 3	Templemore	Londonderry Urban No. 1	Londonderry	Irish Society
Londonderry, Horsebarrack Row	Londonderry Urban No. 3	Templemore	Londonderry Urban No. 1	Londonderry	Irish Society
Londonderry, Howard Place	Londonderry Urban No. 4	Templemore	Londonderry Urban No. 2	Londonderry	Irish Society

Townland	D.E.D.	Parish	Registrar District	Poor Law Union	17th Century Landowner
Londonderry, Howard Street	Londonderry Urban No. 4	Templemore	Londonderry Urban No. 2	Londonderry	Irish Society
Londonderry, Howard Street	Londonderry Urban No. 2	Templemore	Londonderry Urban No. 2	Londonderry	Irish Society
Londonderry, Infirmary Road	Londonderry Urban No. 1	Templemore	Londonderry Urban No. 2	Londonderry	Irish Society
Londonderry, Infirmary Road	Londonderry Urban No. 1	Templemore	Londonderry Urban No. 2	Londonderry	Irish Society
Londonderry, Irish Street	Waterside	Clondermot	Waterside Urban	Londonderry	Irish Society
Londonderry, Ivy Terrace	Londonderry Urban No. 2	Templemore	Londonderry Urban No. 1	Londonderry	Irish Society
Londonderry, John Street	Londonderry Urban No. 3	Templemore	Londonderry Urban No. 1	Londonderry	Irish Society
Londonderry, Joseph Street	Londonderry Urban No. 4	Templemore	Londonderry Urban No. 2	Londonderry	Irish Society
Londonderry, Kennedy Place	Londonderry Urban No. 3	Templemore	Londonderry Urban No. 1	Londonderry	Irish Society
Londonderry, Kennedy Street	Londonderry Urban No. 3	Templemore	Londonderry Urban No. 1	Londonderry	Irish Society
Londonderry, Lawrence Street	Londonderry Urban No. 1	Templemore	Londonderry Urban No. 2	Londonderry	Irish Society
Londonderry, Lecky Road	Londonderry Urban No. 4	Templemore	Londonderry Urban No. 2	Londonderry	Irish Society
Londonderry, Lecky Road	Londonderry Urban No. 4	Templemore	Londonderry Urban No. 2	Londonderry	Irish Society
Londonderry, Lecky Road	Londonderry Urban No. 2	Templemore	Londonderry Urban No. 2	Londonderry	Irish Society
Londonderry, Lewis Street	Londonderry Urban No. 1	Templemore	Londonderry Urban No. 2	Londonderry	Irish Society
Londonderry, Linenhall Street	Londonderry Urban No. 3	Templemore	Londonderry Urban No. 1	Londonderry	Irish Society
Londonderry, Little Diamond	Londonderry Urban No. 4	Templemore	Londonderry Urban No. 2	Londonderry	Irish Society
Londonderry, Little James Street	Londonderry Urban No. 1	Templemore	Londonderry Urban No. 2	Londonderry	Irish Society
Londonderry, London Street	Londonderry Urban No. 3	Templemore	Londonderry Urban No. 1	Londonderry	Irish Society
Londonderry, Lone Moor Road	Londonderry Urban No. 1	Templemore	Londonderry Urban No. 2	Londonderry	Irish Society
Londonderry, Lone Moor Road	Londonderry Urban No. 4	Templemore	Londonderry Urban No. 2	Londonderry	Irish Society
Londonderry, Lone Moor Road	Londonderry Urban No. 2	Templemore	Londonderry Urban No. 2	Londonderry	Irish Society
Londonderry, Long Tower	Londonderry Urban No. 4	Templemore	Londonderry Urban No. 2	Londonderry	Irish Society
Londonderry, Long Tower Street	Londonderry Urban No. 2	Templemore	Londonderry Urban No. 2	Londonderry	Irish Society
Londonderry, Lorne Street	Londonderry Urban No. 3	Templemore	Londonderry Urban No. 1	Londonderry	Irish Society
Londonderry, Lower Road	Londonderry Urban No. 1	Templemore	Londonderry Urban No. 2	Londonderry	Irish Society
Londonderry, Lundy's Lane	Londonderry Urban No. 2	Templemore	Londonderry Urban No. 2	Londonderry	Irish Society
Londonderry, Magazine Street	Londonderry Urban No. 1	Templemore	Londonderry Urban No. 2	Londonderry	Irish Society

Townland	D.E.D.	Parish	Registrar District	Poor Law Union	17th Century Landowner
Londonderry, Magazine Street	Londonderry Urban No. 4	Templemore	Londonderry Urban No. 2	Londonderry	Irish Society
Londonderry, Major's Row	Londonderry Urban No. 3	Templemore	Londonderry Urban No. 1	Londonderry	Irish Society
Londonderry, Maple Street	Waterside	Clondermot	Waterside Urban	Londonderry	Irish Society
Londonderry, Margaret Street	Waterside	Clondermot	Waterside Urban	Londonderry	Irish Society
Londonderry, Market Street	Londonderry Urban No. 3	Templemore	Londonderry Urban No. 1	Londonderry	Irish Society
Londonderry, Marlborough Avenue	Londonderry Urban No. 1	Templemore	Londonderry Urban No. 2	Londonderry	Irish Society
Londonderry, Marlborough Street	Londonderry Urban No. 1	Templemore	Londonderry Urban No. 2	Londonderry	Irish Society
Londonderry, Marshall's Close	Londonderry Urban No. 1	Templemore	Londonderry Urban No. 2	Londonderry	Irish Society
Londonderry, Matty's Lane	Londonderry Urban No. 3	Templemore	Londonderry Urban No. 1	Londonderry	Irish Society
Londonderry, May Street	Waterside	Clondermot	Waterside Urban	Londonderry	Irish Society
Londonderry, McLoughlin's Close	Waterside	Clondermot	Waterside Urban	Londonderry	Irish Society
Londonderry, McLoughlin's Close	Londonderry Urban No. 2	Templemore	Londonderry Urban No. 1	Londonderry	Irish Society
Londonderry, Meadowbank Avenue	Londonderry Urban No. 1	Templemore	Londonderry Urban No. 2	Londonderry	Irish Society
Londonderry, Meehan's Row	Waterside	Clondermot	Waterside Urban	Londonderry	Irish Society
Londonderry, Mews Lane	Londonderry Urban No. 1	Templemore	Londonderry Urban No. 2	Londonderry	Irish Society
Londonderry, Miaden's Row	Londonderry Urban No. 4	Templemore	Londonderry Urban No. 2	Londonderry	Irish Society
Londonderry, Mill Street	Waterside	Clondermot	Waterside Urban	Londonderry	Irish Society
Londonderry, Millar's Close	Londonderry Urban No. 3	Templemore	Londonderry Urban No. 1	Londonderry	Irish Society
Londonderry, Miller Street	Londonderry Urban No. 2	Templemore	Londonderry Urban No. 1	Londonderry	Irish Society
Londonderry, Moat Street	Londonderry Urban No. 2	Templemore	Londonderry Urban No. 1	Londonderry	Irish Society
Londonderry, Montgomery Street	Londonderry Urban No. 1	Templemore	Londonderry Urban No. 2	Londonderry	Irish Society
Londonderry, Moore Street	Waterside	Clondermot	Waterside Urban	Londonderry	Irish Society
Londonderry, Moore Street	Londonderry Urban No. 2	Templemore	Londonderry Urban No. 2	Londonderry	Irish Society
Londonderry, Morrison's Close	Londonderry Urban No. 4	Templemore	Londonderry Urban No. 2	Londonderry	Irish Society
Londonderry, Mountjoy Street	Londonderry Urban No. 2	Templemore	Londonderry Urban No. 1	Londonderry	Irish Society

Townland	D.E.D.	Parish	Registrar District	Poor Law Union	17th Century Landowner
Londonderry, Nailor's Row	Londonderry Urban No. 4	Templemore	Londonderry Urban No. 2	Londonderry	Irish Society
Londonderry, Nassau Street Lower	Londonderry Urban No. 1	Templemore	Londonderry Urban No. 2	Londonderry	Irish Society
Londonderry, Nassau Street Upper	Londonderry Urban No. 1	Templemore	Londonderry Urban No. 2	Londonderry	Irish Society
Londonderry, Nelson Street	Londonderry Urban No. 4	Templemore	Londonderry Urban No. 2	Londonderry	Irish Society
Londonderry, New Market Street	Londonderry Urban No. 3	Templemore	Londonderry Urban No. 1	Londonderry	Irish Society
Londonderry, New Row	Londonderry Urban No. 1	Templemore	Londonderry Urban No. 2	Londonderry	Irish Society
Londonderry, New Street	Waterside	Clondermot	Waterside Urban	Londonderry	Irish Society
Londonderry, New Street	Waterside	Clondermot	Waterside Urban	Londonderry	Irish Society
Londonderry, Nicholson Square	Londonderry Urban No. 1	Templemore	Londonderry Urban No. 2	Londonderry	Irish Society
Londonderry, Nicholson Terrace	Londonderry Urban No. 1	Templemore	Londonderry Urban No. 2	Londonderry	Irish Society
Londonderry, North Edward Street	Londonderry Urban No. 1	Templemore	Londonderry Urban No. 2	Londonderry	Irish Society
Londonderry, Northland Avenue	Londonderry Urban No. 1	Templemore	Londonderry Urban No. 2	Londonderry	Irish Society
Londonderry, Northland Road	Londonderry Urban No. 1	Templemore	Londonderry Urban No. 2	Londonderry	Irish Society
Londonderry, Northland Road	Londonderry Urban No. 1	Templemore	Londonderry Urban No. 2	Londonderry	Irish Society
Londonderry, Oakum Alley	Londonderry Urban No. 3	Templemore	Londonderry Urban No. 1	Londonderry	Irish Society
Londonderry, Orchard Lane	Londonderry Urban No. 3	Templemore	Londonderry Urban No. 1	Londonderry	Irish Society
Londonderry, Orchard Row	Londonderry Urban No. 2	Templemore	Londonderry Urban No. 1	Londonderry	Irish Society
Londonderry, Orchard Street	Londonderry Urban No. 3	Templemore	Londonderry Urban No. 1	Londonderry	Irish Society
Londonderry, Osborne Street	Londonderry Urban No. 1	Templemore	Londonderry Urban No. 2	Londonderry	Irish Society
Londonderry, Palace Street	Londonderry Urban No. 4	Templemore	Londonderry Urban No. 2	Londonderry	Irish Society
Londonderry, Park Avenue	Londonderry Urban No. 1	Templemore	Londonderry Urban No. 2	Londonderry	Irish Society
Londonderry, Park Terrace	Londonderry Urban No. 1	Templemore	Londonderry Urban No. 2	Londonderry	Irish Society
Londonderry, Patrick Street	Londonderry Urban No. 1	Templemore	Londonderry Urban No. 2	Londonderry	Irish Society
Londonderry, Phillips Street	Londonderry Urban No. 1	Templemore	Londonderry Urban No. 2	Londonderry	Irish Society
Londonderry, Pilots' Row	Londonderry Urban No. 4	Templemore	Londonderry Urban No. 2	Londonderry	Irish Society
Londonderry, Pine Street	Waterside	Clondermot	Waterside Urban	Londonderry	Irish Society
Londonderry, Pitt Street	Londonderry Urban No. 2	Templemore	Londonderry Urban No. 2	Londonderry	Irish Society

Townland	D.E.D.	Parish	Registrar District	Poor Law Union	17th Century Landowner
Londonderry, Platt's Close	Londonderry Urban No. 3	Templemore	Londonderry Urban No. 1	Londonderry	Irish Society
Londonderry, Port of Londonderry	Londonderry Urban No. 3	Templemore	Londonderry Urban No. 1	Londonderry	Irish Society
Londonderry, Port Shipping Return	Londonderry Urban No. 1	Templemore	Londonderry Urban No. 2	Londonderry	Irish Society
Londonderry, Prince Arthur Street	Londonderry Urban No. 1	Templemore	Londonderry Urban No. 2	Londonderry	Irish Society
Londonderry, Prince's Quay	Londonderry Urban No. 3	Templemore	Londonderry Urban No. 1	Londonderry	Irish Society
Londonderry, Princes Street	Londonderry Urban No. 1	Templemore	Londonderry Urban No. 2	Londonderry	Irish Society
Londonderry, Princes Terrace	Londonderry Urban No. 1	Templemore	Londonderry Urban No. 2	Londonderry	Irish Society
Londonderry, Pump Street	Londonderry Urban No. 3	Templemore	Londonderry Urban No. 1	Londonderry	Irish Society
Londonderry, Quarry Street	Londonderry Urban No. 2	Templemore	Londonderry Urban No. 2	Londonderry	Irish Society
Londonderry, Queen Street	Londonderry Urban No. 1	Templemore	Londonderry Urban No. 2	Londonderry	Irish Society
Queen's Quay	Urban No. 1		Urban No. 2		
Londonderry, Richmond Street	Londonderry Urban No. 3	Templemore	Londonderry Urban No. 1	Londonderry	Irish Society
Londonderry, Riverview Terrace	Waterside	Clondermot	Waterside Urban	Londonderry	Irish Society
Londonderry, Rosemount Avenue	Londonderry Urban No. 1	Templemore	Londonderry Urban No. 2	Londonderry	Irish Society
Londonderry, Rosemount Avenue	Londonderry Urban No. 1	Templemore	Londonderry Urban No. 2	Londonderry	Irish Society
Londonderry, Rosemount Terrace	Londonderry Urban No. 1	Templemore	Londonderry Urban No. 2	Londonderry	Irish Society
Londonderry, Rossville Street	Londonderry Urban No. 4	Templemore	Londonderry Urban No. 2	Londonderry	Irish Society
Londonderry, Rossville Street	Londonderry Urban No. 4	Templemore	Londonderry Urban No. 2	Londonderry	Irish Society
Londonderry, Sackville Street	Londonderry Urban No. 1	Templemore	Londonderry Urban No. 2	Londonderry	Irish Society
Londonderry, Shipquay Place	Londonderry Urban No. 3	Templemore	Londonderry Urban No. 1	Londonderry	Irish Society
Londonderry, Shipquay Steet	Londonderry Urban No. 4	Templemore	Londonderry Urban No. 2	Londonderry	Irish Society
Londonderry, Shipquay Street	Londonderry Urban No. 3	Templemore	Londonderry Urban No. 1	Londonderry	Irish Society
Londonderry, Shipquay Street	Londonderry Urban No. 1	Templemore	Londonderry Urban No. 2	Londonderry	Irish Society
Londonderry, Simpson's Brae	Waterside	Clondermot	Waterside Urban	Londonderry	Irish Society
Londonderry, Sloan's Terrace	Londonderry Urban No. 2	Templemore	Londonderry Urban No. 1	Londonderry	Irish Society
Londonderry, Society Street	Londonderry Urban No. 4	Templemore	Londonderry Urban No. 2	Londonderry	Irish Society

Townland	D.E.D.	Parish	Registrar District	Poor Law Union	17th Century Landowner
Londonderry, Spencer Road	Waterside	Clondermot	Waterside Urban	Londonderry	Irish Society
Londonderry, St Columb's Court	Londonderry Urban No. 3	Templemore	Londonderry Urban No. 1	Londonderry	Irish Society
Londonderry, St Columb's Street	Londonderry Urban No. 4	Templemore	Londonderry Urban No. 2	Londonderry	Irish Society
Londonderry, St Columb's Wells	Londonderry Urban No. 4	Templemore	Londonderry Urban No. 2	Londonderry	Irish Society
Londonderry, St Columb's Wells	Londonderry Urban No. 2	Templemore	Londonderry Urban No. 2	Londonderry	Irish Society
Londonderry, St Patrick's Street	Londonderry Urban No. 4	Templemore	Londonderry Urban No. 2	Londonderry	Irish Society
Londonderry, Stable Lane	Londonderry Urban No. 4	Templemore	Londonderry Urban No. 2	Londonderry	Irish Society
Londonderry, Stanley's Walk	Londonderry Urban No. 4	Templemore	Londonderry Urban No. 2	Londonderry	Irish Society
Londonderry, Stewart's Close	Londonderry Urban No. 1	Templemore	Londonderry Urban No. 2	Londonderry	Irish Society
Londonderry, Stewart's Terrace	Londonderry Urban No. 1	Templemore	Londonderry Urban No. 2	Londonderry	Irish Society
Londonderry, Strabane Old Road	Waterside	Clondermot	Waterside Urban	Londonderry	Irish Society
Londonderry, Strand Road	Londonderry Urban No. 1	Templemore	Londonderry Urban No. 2	Londonderry	Irish Society
Londonderry, Sugarhouse Lane	Londonderry Urban No. 3	Templemore	Londonderry Urban No. 1	Londonderry	Irish Society
Londonderry, Templemore Park	Londonderry Urban No. 1	Templemore	Londonderry Urban No. 2	Londonderry	Irish Society
Londonderry, Templemore Street	Londonderry Urban No. 2	Templemore	Londonderry Urban No. 2	Londonderry	Irish Society
Londonderry, Templemore Terrace	Londonderry Urban No. 1	Templemore	Londonderry Urban No. 2	Londonderry	Irish Society
Londonderry, Termon Street	Waterside	Clondermot	Waterside Urban	Londonderry	Irish Society
Londonderry, Thomas Street	Londonderry Urban No. 4	Templemore	Londonderry Urban No. 2	Londonderry	Irish Society
Londonderry, Townsend Street	Londonderry Urban No. 2	Templemore	Londonderry Urban No. 2	Londonderry	Irish Society
Londonderry, Union Street	Waterside	Clondermot	Waterside Urban	Londonderry	Irish Society
Londonderry, Union Street	Londonderry Urban No. 4	Templemore	Londonderry Urban No. 2	Londonderry	Irish Society
Londonderry, Victoria Park	Waterside	Clondermot	Waterside Urban	Londonderry	Irish Society
Londonderry, Victoria Place	Londonderry Urban No. 2	Templemore	Londonderry Urban No. 1	Londonderry	Irish Society
Londonderry, Victoria Road	Waterside	Clondermot	Waterside Urban	Londonderry	Irish Society
Londonderry, Victoria Street	Londonderry Urban No. 3	Templemore	Londonderry Urban No. 1	Londonderry	Irish Society
Londonderry, Violet Street	Waterside	Clondermot	Waterside Urban	Londonderry	Irish Society
Londonderry, Walker's Place	Waterside	Clondermot	Waterside Urban	Londonderry	Irish Society
Londonderry, Walker's Place	Londonderry Urban No. 4	Templemore	Londonderry Urban No. 2	Londonderry	Irish Society

Townland	D.E.D.	Parish	Registrar District	Poor Law Union	17th Century Landowner
Londonderry, Wapping Lane	Londonderry Urban No. 3	Templemore	Londonderry Urban No. 1	Londonderry	Irish Society
Londonderry, Wapping Lane	Londonderry Urban No. 3	Templemore	Londonderry Urban No. 1	Londonderry	Irish Society
Londonderry, Water Street	Londonderry Urban No. 3	Templemore	Londonderry Urban No. 1	Londonderry	Irish Society
Londonderry, Waterloo Place	Londonderry Urban No. 1	Templemore	Londonderry Urban No. 2	Londonderry	Irish Society
Londonderry, Waterloo Street	Londonderry Urban No. 1	Templemore	Londonderry Urban No. 2	Londonderry	Irish Society
Londonderry, Waterloo Street	Londonderry Urban No. 4	Templemore	Londonderry Urban No. 2	Londonderry	Irish Society
Londonderry, Waterside Quay	Waterside	Clondermot	Waterside Urban	Londonderry	Irish Society
Londonderry, Wellington Street	Londonderry Urban No. 4	Templemore	Londonderry Urban No. 2	Londonderry	Irish Society
Londonderry, West End Park	Londonderry Urban No. 1	Templemore	Londonderry Urban No. 2	Londonderry	Irish Society
Londonderry, Whittaker Street	Londonderry Urban No. 3	Templemore	Londonderry Urban No. 1	Londonderry	Irish Society
Londonderry, Whittaker Street	Londonderry Urban No. 1	Templemore	Londonderry Urban No. 2	Londonderry	Irish Society
Londonderry, William Street	Londonderry Urban No. 1	Templemore	Londonderry Urban No. 2	Londonderry	Irish Society
Londonderry, William Street	Londonderry Urban No. 4	Templemore	Londonderry Urban No. 2	Londonderry	Irish Society
Londonderry, William Street	Londonderry Urban No. 4	Templemore	Londonderry Urban No. 2	Londonderry	Irish Society
Londonderry, Windmill Terrace	Londonderry Urban No. 2	Templemore	Londonderry Urban No. 2	Londonderry	Irish Society
Londonderry, Workhouse	Waterside	Clondermot	Waterside Urban	Londonderry	Irish Society
Longfield	Iniscarn	Desertmartin	Draperstown	Magherafelt	Drapers
Longfield Beg	Eglinton	Faughanvale	Eglinton	Londonderry	Grocers
Longfield Level	Eglinton	Faughanvale	Eglinton	Londonderry	Grocers
Longfield More	Eglinton	Faughanvale	Eglinton	Londonderry	Grocers
Long's Glebe	Downhill	Dunboe	Articlave	Coleraine	Churchland
Loughan Hill	Ballylagan	Coleraine	Portstewart	Coleraine	Irish Society
Loughanreagh North	Knockantern	Kildollagh	Coleraine	Coleraine	Irish Society
Loughanreagh South	Knockantern	Kildollagh	Coleraine	Coleraine	Irish Society
Loughermore	Ballykelly	Faughanvale	Ballykelly	Limavady	Fishmongers
Loughtilube	Banagher	Learmount	Claudy	Londonderry	Skinners
Luney	Desertmartin	Desertmartin	Magherafelt	Magherafelt	Vintners
Lurganagoose	Rocktown	Termoneeny	Bellaghy	Magherafelt	Vintners
Macfinn Lower	Knockantern	Ballymoney	Coleraine	Coleraine	Earl of Antrim
Macknagh	Swatragh	Maghera	Maghera	Magherafelt	Mercers
Macleary	Drumcroon	Macosquin	Aghadowey	Coleraine	Merchant Taylors
Macosquin	Drumcroon	Macosquin	Aghadowey	Coleraine	Churchland
Maddybenny Beg	Portstewart	Ballyaghran	Portstewart	Coleraine	Irish Society

Townland	D.E.D.	Parish	Registrar District	Poor Law Union	17th Century Landowner
Maddybenny More	Portstewart	Ballyaghran	Portstewart	Coleraine	Irish Society
Maghadone	The Loup	Artrea	Moneymore	Magherafelt	Salters
Maghera town	Maghera	Maghera	Maghera	Magherafelt	Churchland
Magheraboy	Ballylagan	Ballywillin	Portstewart	Coleraine	Irish Society
Magheraboy	Dungiven	Dungiven	Dungiven	Limavady	Skinners
Magheracanon	Glendermot	Clondermot	Waterside Rural	Londonderry	Goldsmiths
Magheraclay	Portstewart	Ballyaghran	Portstewart	Coleraine	Irish Society
Magherafelt, Broad Street	Magherafelt	Magherafelt	Magherafelt	Magherafelt	Salters
Magherafelt, Church Street	Magherafelt	Magherafelt	Magherafelt	Magherafelt	Salters
Magherafelt, Garden Street	Magherafelt	Magherafelt	Magherafelt	Magherafelt	Salters
Magherafelt, King Street	Magherafelt	Magherafelt	Magherafelt	Magherafelt	Salters
Magherafelt, Market Street	Magherafelt	Magherafelt	Magherafelt	Magherafelt	Salters
Magherafelt, Meeting Street	Magherafelt	Magherafelt	Magherafelt	Magherafelt	Salters
Magherafelt, Queen Street	Magherafelt	Magherafelt	Magherafelt	Magherafelt	Salters
Magherafelt, Rainey Street	Magherafelt	Magherafelt	Magherafelt	Magherafelt	Salters
Magherafelt, Station Road	Magherafelt	Magherafelt	Magherafelt	Magherafelt	Salters
Magherafelt, Union Road	Magherafelt	Magherafelt	Magherafelt	Magherafelt	Salters
Magheramenagh	Ballylagan	Ballywillin	Portstewart	Coleraine	Irish Society
Magheramore	Owenreagh	Banagher	Feeny	Limavady	Churchland
Magheramore	Slaght	Desertoghill	Garvagh	Coleraine	Ironmongers
Magheramore	Faughanvale	Faughanvale	Ballykelly	Limavady	Fishmongers
Magheramore	The Highlands	Tamlaght Finlagan	Ballykelly	Limavady	Phillips
Magherascullion	Moneymore	Desertlyn	Moneymore	Magherafelt	Drapers
Magheraskeagh	Aghanloo	Aghanloo	Bellarena	Limavady	Haberdashers
Maine North	Lislane	Balteagh	Limavady	Limavady	Haberdashers
Maine South	Lislane	Carrick	Limavady	Limavady	Haberdashers
Managh Beg	Lough Enagh	Clondermot	Eglinton	Londonderry	Grocers
Managh More	Lough Enagh	Clondermot	Eglinton	Londonderry	Grocers
Managher	Somerset	Aghadowey	Aghadowey	Coleraine	Ironmongers
Margymonaghan	Bellarena	Magilligan	Bellarena	Limavady	Churchland
Masteragwee	Bannbrook	Dunboe	Articlave	Coleraine	Churchland
Mawillian	Springhill	Artrea	Moneymore	Magherafelt	Salters
Mayboy	Glenkeen	Aghadowey	Garvagh	Coleraine	Ironmongers
Mayboy	Glenkeen	Errigal	Garvagh	Coleraine	Ironmongers
Maydown	Lough Enagh	Clondermot	Eglinton	Londonderry	Grocers
Mayoghill	Bovagh	Aghadowey	Garvagh	Coleraine	Ironmongers
McLean and Partners Division	Eglinton	Faughanvale	Eglinton	Londonderry	Grocers

Townland	D.E.D.	Parish	Registrar District	Poor Law Union	17th Century Landowner
Meavemanougher	Ringsend	Aghadowey	Aghadowey	Coleraine	Merchant Taylors
Meencraig	Ringsend	Aghadowey	Aghadowey	Coleraine	Merchant Taylors
Meencraig	Ringsend	Errigal	Aghadowey	Coleraine	Merchant Taylors
Megargy	Ballymoghan	Magherafelt	Magherafelt	Magherafelt	Salters
Menagh	Aghadowey	Aghadowey	Aghadowey	Coleraine	Churchland
Mettican Glebe	Garvagh	Errigal	Garvagh	Coleraine	Churchland
Mill Loughan	Knockantern	Kildollagh	Coleraine	Coleraine	Irish Society
Milltown	Bellarena	Magilligan	Bellarena	Limavady	Churchland
Minearny	Bellarena	Magilligan	Bellarena	Limavady	Churchland
Minegallagher Glebe	Faughanvale	Faughanvale	Ballykelly	Limavady	Churchland
Mobuoy	Lough Enagh	Faughanvale	Eglinton	Londonderry	Grocers
Mobuy	Lissan Upper	Lissan	Moneymore	Magherafelt	Churchland
Monehanegan	Eglinton	Faughanvale	Eglinton	Londonderry	Grocers
Moneybrannon	Aghadowey	Aghadowey	Aghadowey	Coleraine	Churchland
Moneycarrie Lower	Aghadowey	Aghadowey	Aghadowey	Coleraine	Churchland
Moneycarrie Upper	Aghadowey	Aghadowey	Aghadowey	Coleraine	Churchland
Moneyconey	The Six Towns	Ballynascreen	Draperstown	Magherafelt	Churchland
Moneydig	Bovagh	Desertoghill	Garvagh	Coleraine	Ironmongers
Moneygran	Kilrea	Kilrea	Kilrea	Coleraine	Mercers
Moneyguiggy	Carnamoney	Ballynascreen	Draperstown	Magherafelt	Drapers
Moneyguiggy	Lislane	Balteagh	Limavady	Limavady	Haberdashers
Moneyhaw	Moneyhaw	Arboe	Moneymore	Magherafelt	Drapers
Moneyhaw	Moneyhaw	Lissan	Moneymore	Magherafelt	Drapers
Moneyhoghan	Banagher	Learmount	Claudy	Londonderry	Skinners
Moneymore	Moneymore	Artrea	Moneymore	Magherafelt	Drapers
Moneymore	Moneymore	Desertlyn	Moneymore	Magherafelt	Drapers
Moneymore	Maghera	Maghera	Maghera	Magherafelt	Churchland
Moneymore, Bridge Street	Moneymore	Artrea	Moneymore	Magherafelt	Drapers
Moneymore, Cunningham Street	Moneymore	Artrea	Moneymore	Magherafelt	Drapers
Moneymore, Hammond Road	Moneymore	Artrea	Moneymore	Magherafelt	Drapers
Moneymore, Hammond Street	Moneymore	Artrea	Moneymore	Magherafelt	Drapers
Moneymore, High Street	Moneymore	Artrea	Moneymore	Magherafelt	Drapers
Moneymore, Lawford Street	Moneymore	Artrea	Moneymore	Magherafelt	Drapers
Moneymore, Lawford Street	Moneymore	Desertlyn	Moneymore	Magherafelt	Drapers
Moneymore, Smith Street	Moneymore	Desertlyn	Moneymore	Magherafelt	Drapers

Townland	D.E.D.	Parish	Registrar District	Poor Law Union	17th Century Landowner
Moneymore, Stonard Street	Moneymore	Artrea	Moneymore	Magherafelt	Drapers
Moneyneany	Draperstown	Ballynascreen	Draperstown	Magherafelt	Drapers
Moneyrannel	Fruithill	Tamlaght Finlagan	Limavady	Limavady	Churchland
Moneysallin	Tamlaght	Tamlaght O'Crilly	Kilrea	Coleraine	Mercers
Moneyshanere	Tobermore	Kilcronaghan	Maghera	Magherafelt	Drapers
Moneysharvan	Swatragh	Killelagh	Maghera	Magherafelt	Mercers
Moneystaghan Ellis	Clady	Tamlaght O'Crilly	Bellaghy	Magherafelt	Vintners
Moneystaghan Macpeake	Clady	Tamlaght O'Crilly	Bellaghy	Magherafelt	Vintners
Monnaboy	Eglinton	Faughanvale	Eglinton	Londonderry	Grocers
Mormeal	Tobermore	Kilcronaghan	Maghera	Magherafelt	Churchland
Motalee	Desertmartin	Desertmartin	Magherafelt	Magherafelt	Vintners
Mount Sandel	Knockantern	Coleraine	Coleraine	Coleraine	Irish Society
Movanagher	Kilrea	Kilrea	Kilrea	Coleraine	Mercers
Movenis	Bovagh	Desertoghill	Garvagh	Coleraine	Ironmongers
Moyagall	Gulladuff	Maghera	Maghera	Magherafelt	Vintners
Moyagoney	Tamlaght	Kilrea	Kilrea	Coleraine	Vintners
Moyard	The Six Towns	Ballynascreen	Draperstown	Magherafelt	Churchland
Moybeg Kirley	Carnamoney	Kilcronaghan	Draperstown	Magherafelt	Drapers
Moydamlaght	Draperstown	Ballynascreen	Draperstown	Magherafelt	Drapers
Moyesset	Tobermore	Kilcronaghan	Maghera	Magherafelt	Drapers
Moyheeland	Draperstown	Ballynascreen	Draperstown	Magherafelt	Drapers
Moykeeran	Draperstown	Ballynascreen	Draperstown	Magherafelt	Drapers
Moyknock	Kilrea	Kilrea	Kilrea	Coleraine	Mercers
Moyletra Kill	Garvagh	Desertoghill	Garvagh	Coleraine	Churchland
Moyletra Toy	The Grove	Desertoghill	Kilrea	Coleraine	Mercers
Moymucklemurry	Ballymoghan	Desertlyn	Magherafelt	Magherafelt	Salters
Moys	The Highlands	Carrick	Ballykelly	Limavady	Phillips
Muff	Eglinton	Faughanvale	Eglinton	Londonderry	Grocers
Muff	Lissan Upper	Lissan	Moneymore	Magherafelt	Churchland
Muff town [Eglinton from 1858]	Eglinton	Faughanvale	Eglinton	Londonderry	Grocers
Mulderg	Foreglen	Cumber Upper	Feeny	Limavady	Fishmongers
Muldonagh	Drum	Bovevagh	Dungiven	Limavady	Phillips
Mulkeeragh	Gelvin	Bovevagh	Dungiven	Limavady	Haberdashers
Mulkeeragh	Ballykelly	Tamlaght Finlagan	Ballykelly	Limavady	Churchland
Mullaboy	Tamnaherin	Cumber Lower	Eglinton	Londonderry	Grocers
Mullagh	Fruithill	Tamlaght Finlagan	Limavady	Limavady	Phillips
Mullagh	Maghera	Termoneeny	Maghera	Magherafelt	Churchland
Mullaghacall North	Portstewart	Ballyaghran	Portstewart	Coleraine	Irish Society

Townland	D.E.D.	Parish	Registrar District	Poor Law Union	17th Century Landowner
Mullaghacall South	Portstewart	Ballyaghran	Portstewart	Coleraine	Irish Society
Mullaghboy	Bellaghy	Ballyscullion	Bellaghy	Magherafelt	Vintners
Mullaghboy	Magherafelt	Magherafelt	Magherafelt	Magherafelt	Salters
Mullaghinch	Agivey	Aghadowey	Aghadowey	Coleraine	Ironmongers
Mullaghmore	Agivey	Agivey	Aghadowey	Coleraine	Ironmongers
Mullaghmore Glebe	Agivey	Agivey	Aghadowey	Coleraine	Churchland
Mullaghnamoyagh	Clady	Tamlaght O'Crilly	Bellaghy	Magherafelt	Churchland
Mullamore Town	Agivey	Aghadowey	Aghadowey	Coleraine	Ironmongers
Mullan	Aghadowey	Aghadowey	Aghadowey	Coleraine	Churchland
Mullan	Kilrea	Kilrea	Kilrea	Coleraine	Mercers
Mullane	Fruithill	Drumachose	Limavady	Limavady	Churchland
Mullanhead	Bannbrook	Dunboe	Articlave	Coleraine	Churchland
Mullennan	Liberties Upper	Templemore	Liberties Upper	Londonderry	Irish Society
Mullinabrone	Bovagh	Aghadowey	Garvagh	Coleraine	Churchland
Mulnavoo	Draperstown	Ballynascreen	Draperstown	Magherafelt	Skinners
Myroe Level	Myroe	Tamlaght Finlagan	Bellarena	Limavady	Phillips
Nare	Portstewart	Ballyaghran	Portstewart	Coleraine	Irish Society
Ned	Ballykelly	Tamlaght Finlagan	Ballykelly	Limavady	Fishmongers
Oghill	Tamnaherin	Cumber Lower	Eglinton	Londonderry	Grocers
Oghill	Ballykelly	Tamlaght Finlagan	Ballykelly	Limavady	Fishmongers
Old Town Deer Park	Bellaghy	Ballyscullion	Bellaghy	Magherafelt	Vintners
Old Town Downing	Bellaghy	Ballyscullion	Bellaghy	Magherafelt	Vintners
One Other Island	Castle Dawson	Ballyscullion	Bellaghy	Magherafelt	Phillips
Oughtagh	Tamnaherin	Cumber Lower	Eglinton	Londonderry	Grocers
Oughtymore	Benone	Magilligan	Bellarena	Limavady	Churchland
Oughtymoyle	Bellarena	Magilligan	Bellarena	Limavady	Churchland
Ovil	Dungiven	Dungiven	Dungiven	Limavady	Skinners
Owenbeg	Dungiven	Dungiven	Dungiven	Limavady	Skinners
Owenreagh	The Six Towns	Ballynascreen	Draperstown	Magherafelt	Churchland
Pennyburn	Londonderry Urban No. 1	Templemore	Londonderry Urban No. 2	Londonderry	Irish Society
Polepatrick	Magherafelt	Magherafelt	Magherafelt	Magherafelt	Salters
Portstewart village (Mullaghacall North)	Portstewart	Ballyaghran	Portstewart	Coleraine	Irish Society
Portstewart village (Tullaghmurry East)	Portstewart	Ballyaghran	Portstewart	Coleraine	Irish Society
Pottagh	Bannbrook	Dunboe	Articlave	Coleraine	Churchland
Prehen	Glendermot	Clondermot	Waterside Rural	Londonderry	Goldsmiths
Primity	Glendermot	Clondermot	Waterside Rural	Londonderry	Goldsmiths

Townland	D.E.D.	Parish	Registrar District	Poor Law Union	17th Century Landowner
Pullans North	Knockantern	Kildollagh	Coleraine	Coleraine	Irish Society
Pullans South	Knockantern	Kildollagh	Coleraine	Coleraine	Irish Society
Quilley Lower	Bannbrook	Dunboe	Articlave	Coleraine	Churchland
Quilley Upper	Bannbrook	Dunboe	Articlave	Coleraine	Churchland
Quilly	Brackagh Slieve Gallion	Desertlyn	Moneymore	Magherafelt	Drapers
Rallagh	Feeny	Banagher	Feeny	Limavady	Churchland
Rascahan	Fruithill	Tamlaght Finlagan	Limavady	Limavady	Fishmongers
Raspberry Hill	Bondsglen	Cumber Upper	Claudy	Londonderry	Skinners
Rathbrady More (part of)	Fruithill	Drumachose	Limavady	Limavady	Phillips
Rathfad	Aghanloo	Aghanloo	Bellarena	Limavady	Churchland
Ree	Agivey	Agivey	Aghadowey	Coleraine	Ironmongers
Ringrash Beg	Bannbrook	Macosquin	Articlave	Coleraine	Clothworkers
Ringrash More	Bannbrook	Macosquin	Articlave	Coleraine	Clothworkers
Risk	Agivey	Aghadowey	Aghadowey	Coleraine	Ironmongers
Rocktown	Rocktown	Maghera	Bellaghy	Magherafelt	Vintners
Roselick Beg	Portstewart	Ballyaghran	Portstewart	Coleraine	Irish Society
Roselick More	Portstewart	Ballyaghran	Portstewart	Coleraine	Irish Society
Rosgarran	Desertmartin	Desertmartin	Magherafelt	Magherafelt	Vintners
Roshure	Ballymoghan	Desertmartin	Magherafelt	Magherafelt	Salters
Rossmore	Lissan Upper	Lissan	Moneymore	Magherafelt	Churchland
Rossnagalliagh	Glendermot	Clondermot	Waterside Rural	Londonderry	Churchland
Ruskey	Keady	Drumachose	Limavady	Limavady	Merchant Taylors
Rusky	Agivey	Aghadowey	Aghadowey	Coleraine	Ironmongers
Rusky Lower	Springhill	Tamlaght	Moneymore	Magherafelt	Churchland
Rusky Upper	Springhill	Tamlaght	Moneymore	Magherafelt	Churchland
Sallowilly	Ballymullins	Cumber Upper	Claudy	Londonderry	Skinners
Salt Works	Eglinton	Faughanvale	Eglinton	Londonderry	Grocers
Scab Island	Castle Dawson	Ballyscullion	Bellaghy	Magherafelt	Phillips
Scalty	Agivey	Aghadowey	Aghadowey	Coleraine	Ironmongers
Sconce	Articlave	Formoyle	Articlave	Coleraine	Clothworkers
Scotchtown	Bellarena	Magilligan	Bellarena	Limavady	Churchland
Scriggan	Dungiven	Dungiven	Dungiven	Limavady	Skinners
Seacon Lower	Knockantern	Ballymoney	Coleraine	Coleraine	Earl of Antrim
Seacon More	Knockantern	Ballymoney	Coleraine	Coleraine	Earl of Antrim
Sesnagh	The Highlands	Tamlaght Finlagan	Ballykelly	Limavady	Phillips
Seygorry	Aghadowey	Aghadowey	Aghadowey	Coleraine	Churchland
Shanemullagh	Castle Dawson	Magherafelt	Bellaghy	Magherafelt	Phillips
Shanlongford	Ringsend	Aghadowey	Aghadowey	Coleraine	Merchant Taylors
Shanlongford	Ringsend	Errigal	Aghadowey	Coleraine	Merchant Taylors

Townland	D.E.D.	Parish	Registrar District	Poor Law Union	17th Century Landowner
Shanreagh	Fruithill	Tamlaght Finlagan	Limavady	Limavady	Churchland
Shantallow	Liberties Lower	Templemore	Liberties Lower	Londonderry	Irish Society
Shanvey	Aghanloo	Aghanloo	Bellarena	Limavady	Churchland
Sherriffs Mountain	Liberties Upper	Templemore	Liberties Upper	Londonderry	Irish Society
Sistrakeel	Ballykelly	Tamlaght Finlagan	Ballykelly	Limavady	Fishmongers
Slaghtaverty	Slaght	Errigal	Garvagh	Coleraine	Ironmongers
Slaghtmanus	Tamnaherin	Cumber Lower	Eglinton	Londonderry	Grocers
Slaghtneill	Tullykeeran	Killelagh	Maghera	Magherafelt	Vintners
Slaghtybogy	Gulladuff	Maghera	Maghera	Magherafelt	Vintners
Slimag	Ballylagan	Ballywillin	Portstewart	Coleraine	Irish Society
Small Island	Castle Dawson	Ballyscullion	Bellaghy	Magherafelt	Phillips
Smulgedon	Lislane	Balteagh	Limavady	Limavady	Haberdashers
Somerset	Somerset	Macosquin	Aghadowey	Coleraine	Merchant Taylors
Spittle Hill	Knockantern	Coleraine	Coleraine	Coleraine	Irish Society
Spring Hill	Liberties Upper	Templemore	Liberties Upper	Londonderry	Irish Society
Spring Town	Liberties Lower	Templemore	Liberties Lower	Londonderry	Irish Society
Stradreagh	Aghanloo	Aghanloo	Bellarena	Limavady	Haberdashers
Stradreagh Beg	Lough Enagh	Clondermot	Eglinton	Londonderry	Grocers
Stradreagh More	Lough Enagh	Clondermot	Eglinton	Londonderry	Churchland
Straid	Banagher	Learmount	Claudy	Londonderry	Fishmongers
Stranagard	Desertmartin	Desertmartin	Magherafelt	Magherafelt	Churchland
Strathall	Tamnaherin	Cumber Lower	Eglinton	Londonderry	Goldsmiths?
Straw	Bancran	Ballynascreen	Draperstown	Magherafelt	Skinners
Straw	Straw	Bovevagh	Ballykelly	Limavady	Phillips
Straw Mountain	Bancran	Ballynascreen	Draperstown	Magherafelt	Skinners
Strawmore	Bancran	Ballynascreen	Draperstown	Magherafelt	Skinners
Streeve	Fruithill	Drumachose	Limavady	Limavady	Phillips
Swatragh	Swatragh	Killelagh	Maghera	Magherafelt	Mercers
Swatragh town	Swatragh	Killelagh	Maghera	Magherafelt	Mercers
Tagharina	Glendermot	Clondermot	Waterside Rural	Londonderry	Goldsmiths
Tamlaght	Kilrea	Aghadowey	Kilrea	Coleraine	Mercers
Tamlaght	Springhill	Tamlaght	Moneymore	Magherafelt	Churchland
Tamlaght	Fruithill	Tamlaght Finlagan	Limavady	Limavady	Churchland
Tamlaght	Bellarena	Magilligan	Bellarena	Limavady	Churchland
Tamlaghtduff	Bellaghy	Ballyscullion	Bellaghy	Magherafelt	Vintners
Tamlaghtmore	Moneyhaw	Derryloran	Moneymore	Magherafelt	Drapers
Tamnadeese	Magherafelt	Magherafelt	Magherafelt	Magherafelt	Salters
Tamnadoey	Ballymoghan	Desertlyn	Magherafelt	Magherafelt	Salters
Tamnagh	Banagher	Learmount	Claudy	Londonderry	Skinners
Tamnaherin	Tamnaherin	Cumber Lower	Eglinton	Londonderry	Grocers

Townland	D.E.D.	Parish	Registrar District	Poor Law Union	17th Century Landowner
Tamnamoney	Somerset	Macosquin	Aghadowey	Coleraine	Merchant Taylors
Tamniaran	Castle Dawson	Ballyscullion	Bellaghy	Magherafelt	Phillips
Tamniarin	Glenshane	Dungiven	Dungiven	Limavady	Skinners
Tamnyagan	Feeny	Banagher	Feeny	Limavady	Skinners
Tamnyaskey	Tobermore	Kilcronaghan	Maghera	Magherafelt	Churchland
Tamnymartin	Maghera	Maghera	Maghera	Magherafelt	Churchland
Tamnymore	Waterside	Clondermot	Waterside Rural	Londonderry	Goldsmiths
Tamnymore	Waterside	Clondermot	Waterside Urban	Londonderry	Goldsmiths
Tamnymore	Tamnaherin	Cumber Lower	Eglinton	Londonderry	Goldsmiths?
Tamnymore	Garvagh	Errigal	Garvagh	Coleraine	Ironmongers
Tamnymullan	Maghera	Maghera	Maghera	Magherafelt	Churchland
Tamnyrankin	The Grove	Desertoghill	Kilrea	Coleraine	Mercers
Tamnyreagh	Tamnaherin	Cumber Lower	Eglinton	Londonderry	Grocers
Tartnakilly	The Highlands	Tamlaght Finlagan	Ballykelly	Limavady	Phillips
Teeavan	Owenreagh	Banagher	Feeny	Limavady	Churchland
Teenaght	Banagher	Learmount	Claudy	Londonderry	Fishmongers
Temain	Lislane	Balteagh	Limavady	Limavady	Haberdashers
Templemoyle	Owenreagh	Banagher	Feeny	Limavady	Churchland
Templemoyle	Straw	Carrick	Ballykelly	Limavady	Phillips
Templemoyle	Eglinton	Faughanvale	Eglinton	Londonderry	Grocers
Templetown	Lough Enagh	Clondermot	Eglinton	Londonderry	Churchland
Termonbacca	Liberties Upper	Templemore	Liberties Upper	Londonderry	Irish Society
Ternamuck	Lislane	Balteagh	Limavady	Limavady	Haberdashers
Terressan	Moneyhaw	Derryloran	Moneymore	Magherafelt	Drapers
Terrydoo Clyde	Lislane	Balteagh	Limavady	Limavady	Haberdashers
Terrydoo Walker	Lislane	Balteagh	Limavady	Limavady	Haberdashers
Terrydreen	Banagher	Learmount	Claudy	Londonderry	Fishmongers
Terrydremont North	Fruithill	Balteagh	Limavady	Limavady	Phillips
Terrydremont South	Fruithill	Balteagh	Limavady	Limavady	Phillips
Terrydrum	The Highlands	Carrick	Ballykelly	Limavady	Phillips
The Creagh (Etre and Otra)	Castle Dawson	Artrea	Bellaghy	Magherafelt	Phillips
Tibarran	Ringsend	Errigal	Aghadowey	Coleraine	Merchant Taylors
Timaconway	The Grove	Tamlaght O'Crilly	Kilrea	Coleraine	Mercers
Tintagh	Lissan Upper	Lissan	Moneymore	Magherafelt	Churchland
Tirbracken	Lough Enagh	Clondermot	Eglinton	Londonderry	Grocers
Tircorran	Aghanloo	Aghanloo	Bellarena	Limavady	Haberdashers
Tircreven	Benone	Magilligan	Bellarena	Limavady	Churchland
Tireighter	Ballymullins	Learmount	Claudy	Londonderry	Skinners
Tirgan	Brackagh Slieve Gallion	Desertmartin	Moneymore	Magherafelt	Drapers

Townland	D.E.D.	Parish	Registrar District	Poor Law Union	17th Century Landowner
Tirgarvil	Swatragh	Maghera	Maghera	Magherafelt	Mercers
Tirglassan	Foreglen	Banagher	Feeny	Limavady	Fishmongers
Tirgoland	Dungiven	Dungiven	Dungiven	Limavady	Skinners
Tirhugh	Swatragh	Killelagh	Maghera	Magherafelt	Mercers
Tirkane	Tullykeeran	Killelagh	Maghera	Magherafelt	Churchland
Tirkeeran	Slaght	Desertoghill	Garvagh	Coleraine	Ironmongers
Tirkeeveny	Glendermot	Clondermot	Waterside Rural	Londonderry	Goldsmiths
Tirmacoy	Faughanvale	Faughanvale	Ballykelly	Limavady	Fishmongers
Tirmaquin	Keady	Drumachose	Limavady	Limavady	Haberdashers
Tirnageeragh	Swatragh	Maghera	Maghera	Magherafelt	Mercers
Tirnony	Tullykeeran	Killelagh	Maghera	Magherafelt	Churchland
Toberhead	Desertmartin	Maghera	Magherafelt	Magherafelt	Vintners
Tobermore	Tobermore	Kilcronaghan	Maghera	Magherafelt	Drapers
Tobermore town	Tobermore	Kilcronaghan	Maghera	Magherafelt	Drapers
Tonaght	Bancran	Ballynascreen	Draperstown	Magherafelt	Skinners
Toneduff	Bondsglen	Cumber Lower	Claudy	Londonderry	Skinners
Town Parks of Magherafelt	Magherafelt	Magherafelt	Magherafelt	Magherafelt	Salters
Tralee	Springhill	Artrea	Moneymore	Magherafelt	Churchland
Trienaltenagh	Garvagh	Desertoghill	Garvagh	Coleraine	Ironmongers
Tullaghmurry East	Portstewart	Ballyaghran	Portstewart	Coleraine	Irish Society
Tullaghmurry West	Portstewart	Ballyaghran	Portstewart	Coleraine	Irish Society
Tullanee	Eglinton	Faughanvale	Eglinton	Londonderry	Grocers
Tullans	Knockantern	Coleraine	Coleraine	Coleraine	Irish Society
Tullintrain	Claudy	Cumber Upper	Claudy	Londonderry	Churchland
Tully	Eglinton	Faughanvale	Eglinton	Londonderry	Grocers
Tully	Ballykelly	Tamlaght Finlagan	Ballykelly	Limavady	Churchland
Tully Lower	Glendermot	Clondermot	Waterside Rural	Londonderry	Goldsmiths
Tully Upper	Glendermot	Clondermot	Waterside Rural	Londonderry	Goldsmiths
Tullyally Lower	Ardmore	Clondermot	Waterside Rural	Londonderry	Grocers
Tullyally Upper	Ardmore	Clondermot	Waterside Rural	Londonderry	Grocers
Tullyarmon	Aghanloo	Aghanloo	Bellarena	Limavady	Haberdashers
Tullyboy	Moneyhaw	Derryloran	Moneymore	Magherafelt	Drapers
Tullybrick	The Six Towns	Ballynascreen	Draperstown	Magherafelt	Churchland
Tullybrisland	Eglinton	Faughanvale	Eglinton	Londonderry	Grocers
Tullyhoe	Ballykelly	Tamlaght Finlagan	Ballykelly	Limavady	Fishmongers
Tullykeeran or Tullyheran	Tullykeeran	Killelagh	Maghera	Magherafelt	Churchland
Tullykeeran Mountain	Tullykeeran	Killelagh	Maghera	Magherafelt	Vintners
Tullylinkisay	Magherafelt	Magherafelt	Magherafelt	Magherafelt	Salters
Tullymain	Faughanvale	Faughanvale	Ballykelly	Limavady	Fishmongers

Townland	D.E.D.	Parish	Registrar District	Poor Law Union	17th Century Landowner
Tullynagee	Brackagh Slieve Gallion	Desertlyn	Moneymore	Magherafelt	Drapers
Tullynure	Lissan Upper	Lissan	Moneymore	Magherafelt	Churchland
Tullyroan	Tobermore	Kilcronaghan	Maghera	Magherafelt	Churchland
Tullyverry	Faughanvale	Faughanvale	Ballykelly	Limavady	Churchland
Turmeel	Dungiven	Dungiven	Dungiven	Limavady	Churchland
Turnaface	Moneymore	Lissan	Moneymore	Magherafelt	Drapers
Turnakibbock	Knockantern	Kildollagh	Coleraine	Coleraine	Irish Society
Twenty Acres	Garvagh	Desertoghill	Garvagh	Coleraine	Churchland
Two Other Islands	Bellaghy	Ballyscullion	Bellaghy	Magherafelt	Phillips
Tyanee	Clady	Tamlaght O'Crilly	Bellaghy	Magherafelt	Vintners
Tygore	Eglinton	Faughanvale	Eglinton	Londonderry	Grocers
Umbra	Benone	Magilligan	Bellarena	Limavady	Churchland
Umrycam	Banagher	Banagher	Claudy	Londonderry	Fishmongers
Upperland	Swatragh	Maghera	Maghera	Magherafelt	Mercers
Walworth	Ballykelly	Faughanvale	Ballykelly	Limavady	Fishmongers
Walworth	Ballykelly	Tamlaght Finlagan	Ballykelly	Limavady	Fishmongers
Warbleshinny	Glendermot	Clondermot	Waterside Rural	Londonderry	Goldsmiths
Waterside	Bannbrook	Killowen	Articlave	Coleraine	Clothworkers
Watt's Town	Knockantern	Coleraine	Coleraine	Coleraine	Irish Society
White House or Ballymagrorty	Liberties Lower	Templemore	Liberties Lower	Londonderry	Irish Society
Whitehill	Eglinton	Faughanvale	Eglinton	Londonderry	Grocers
Windy Hall	Knockantern	Coleraine	Coleraine	Coleraine	Irish Society
Woodtown	Benone	Magilligan	Bellarena	Limavady	Churchland

County Derry Parish Reports

Part Two

The key to unlocking Irish family history origins is the knowledge of place. In tracing your roots in Derry the most important piece of information to treasure, to be gleaned from either family folklore or record sources, is any information as to a place of origin of your ancestors.

From a family historian's perspective the most effective way to view Derry is as a county which is subdivided into parishes and which in turn are subdivided into townlands. County Derry, prior to the 20th century, was administered by 46 civil parishes which contained 1,248 townlands, with an average size of 408 acres.

Identification of the ancestral home in County Derry effectively means identifying the townland your ancestor lived in. The townland is the smallest and most ancient of Irish land divisions. The townland was named at an early period, and it usually referred to a very identifiable landmark in the local area such as a mountain, a bog, an oak forest, a village, a fort or a church.

Townlands vary greatly in area as their size was generally based on the fertility of the land. In Faughanvale Parish, which contains 66 townlands, the fertile lowland townland of Muff is some 318 acres in size, while Killywool which extends into the Loughermore Hills contains 1,471 acres. The townland was loosely based on the ancient Irish land measure called the ballyboe, which means cow townland. As a ballyboe was based on the area that could support a fixed number of cattle, it is not surprising that their size varied depending on land quality.

Many record sources of value, both civil and church, to family historians were compiled and recorded by parish. By mid-19th century, County Derry was subdivided into 46 civil parishes. Realistic genealogical research, in the absence of indexes and databases, generally requires knowledge of the parish in which your ancestor lived.

Each of the following parish reports, in alphabetical order, for County Derry describes and locates the parish, identifies the top ten surnames in mid-19th century and details the major record sources for that parish:
- Church Registers, their religious denomination and commencement dates
- Graveyards and their location in mid-19th century;
- Census Returns and Census Substitutes dating from 1663 to 1911.

Tip to Researchers - by using *A New Genealogical Atlas of Ireland* (2nd edition, Brian Mitchell, Genealogical Publishing Company, Baltimore, 2002) civil parish locations can be translated into Church of Ireland parishes, Roman Catholic parishes and Presbyterian Congregations; and by using *A Guide to Irish Parish Registers* (Brian Mitchell, Genealogical Publishing Company, Baltimore, 1988) civil parish locations can also be translated into a listing of surviving church registers of all denominations and their commencement dates.

AGHADOWEY CIVIL PARISH

County:	Londonderry
Barony:	Coleraine
Diocese:	Derry
Poor Law Union:	Ballymoney & Coleraine
Probate District:	Londonderry
Area:	16,348 acres
Population in 1831:	7,634
Topography:	Bounded on the northeast by the River Bann. Mountainous and barren in the west and fertile in the east this parish lies six miles southwest of the town of Coleraine.
Landowners in 1837:	The Ironmongers' Company was the largest landholder. The Mercers' Co., Bishop of Derry and Rev T Richardson were also proprietors.

RECORD SOURCES

Tithe:	1833
Griffith's Valuation:	1859
Census:	1663 (Hearth Rolls), 1740 (Protestant Householders), 1796 (Flax Lists), 1831, 1901 and 1911.

CHURCH REGISTERS

Church of Ireland:	Pre-1870 none. Now joined with Kilrea
Presbyterian:	Aghadowey – Baptisms from 1855
	Ballylintagh (dissolved 1883) – marriages only from 1872
	Killaig – Baptisms 1805-1856 & from 1860
	Marriages 1836-1843 & from 1865
	(united with 2nd Garvagh or Main Street 1977)
	Ringsend – Baptisms from 1871
Roman Catholic:	Coleraine – Baptisms begin 1843

GRAVEYARDS AND TOWNLANDS WHERE FOUND IN 1859:

Church of Ireland:	Aghadowey
Presbyterian:	Ballylintagh, Ballymenagh, Ballywillin and Killeague

TOP TEN SURNAMES IN 1859 (in descending order):

1= Dempsey and Mullen; 3 Kennedy; 4 Miller; 5 Wilson; 6 Boyd; 7= Smith, Thompson and Young; 10= Blair, Rankin and Stewart

AGHANLOO CIVIL PARISH

County:	Londonderry
Barony:	Keenaght
Diocese:	Derry
Poor Law Union:	NewtownLimavady
Probate District:	Londonderry
Area:	8,251 acres
Population in 1831:	2,159
Topography:	Bounded on the west by the River Roe and to the east by the mountains of Binevenagh (1,250 feet) this parish lies two miles north of the town of Limavady.
Landowners in 1837:	Haberdashers' Company.

RECORD SOURCES

Tithe:	1829
Griffith's Valuation:	1858
Census:	1663 (Hearth Rolls), 1740 (Protestant Householders), 1796 (Flax Lists), 1831, 1901 and 1911.

CHURCH REGISTERS

Church of Ireland:	Pre-1870 none. Now joined with Tamlaghtard 1871
Roman Catholic:	Part Limavady – Baptisms begin 1855; Marriages from 1856 and Burials 1859-1869
	Part Magilligan – Baptisms and marriages begin 1833; Burials 1863-1880.

GRAVEYARDS AND TOWNLANDS WHERE FOUND IN 1858:

Church of Ireland:	Rathfad
	Drumbane

TOP TEN SURNAMES IN 1858 (in descending order):

1 Mullen; 2 Wilson; 3 McCluskey; 4 Martin; 5= McLaughlin and Oliver; 7= Bigham, Lynch, Sherrard, Stewart, Taylor and Turbitt

AGIVEY CIVIL PARISH

County:	Londonderry
Barony:	Coleraine
Diocese:	Derry
Poor Law Union:	Coleraine
Probate District:	Londonderry
Area:	1,725 acres
Population in 1831:	938
Topography:	Situated on the west bank of the River Bann. It is a fertile grange in the parish of Aghadowey, six miles southeast of the town of Coleraine.
Landowners in 1837:	Ironmongers' Company.

RECORD SOURCES

Tithe:	No tithe book as this parish was free from tithe assessment
Griffith's Valuation:	1859
Census:	1796 (Flax Lists), 1831, 1901 and 1911.

CHURCH REGISTERS

Church of Ireland:	Aghadowey - Pre-1870 none. Now joined with Kilrea
Roman Catholic:	Coleraine – Baptisms begin 1843

GRAVEYARDS AND TOWNLANDS WHERE FOUND IN 1859:

Mullaghmore

TOP TEN SURNAMES IN 1859 (in descending order):

1 Boyle; 2 Hunter; 3 McLeese; 4 McElroy; 5= Mitchell, Mullins and Shirley; 8 Dempsey, 9= Doherty, Kane, McDonnell; Maquigg and Thompson

ARBOE CIVIL PARISH

County:	Londonderry and Tyrone
Barony:	Loughinsholin in County Derry
	Dungannon Upper in County Tyrone
Diocese:	Armagh
Poor Law Union:	Magherafelt in County Derry
	Cookstown in County Tyrone
Probate District:	Londonderry in County Derry
	Armagh in County Tyrone
Area:	1,358 acres in County Derry
	32,146 acres in County Tyrone (of which 21,000 acres is Lough Neagh)
Population in 1831:	8,148
Topography:	A fertile parish, in the valley of the Ballinderry River, situated on the western shore of Lough Neagh, 5 miles northeast of the town of Stewartstown.

RECORD SOURCES

Tithe:	1826
Griffith's Valuation:	1859 (Derry), 1860 (Tyrone)
Census:	1663 (Hearth Rolls), 1796 (Flax Lists), 1831, 1901 and 1911.

CHURCH REGISTERS

Church of Ireland:	Baptisms 1775-1813 & from 1824
	Marriages 1773-1812 & from 1825
	Now joined with Ballinderry
Presbyterian:	Ballygoney - Baptisms from 1834 (united with Coagh in 1931)
Roman Catholic:	Ardboe – Baptisms and Marriages from 1827

GRAVEYARDS AND TOWNLANDS WHERE FOUND IN 1860:

	Farsnagh (Tyrone)
Church of Ireland:	Aghacolumb (Tyrone)
Roman Catholic:	Mullanahoe (Tyrone)

TOP TEN SURNAMES IN 1860 (in descending order):

1 Devlin; 2 O'Neill; 3 Quinn; 4 Hagen; 5 McGuigan; 6= Campbell and Corr; 8 Donaghy; 9 McKeon; 10= Donnelly and Hamilton

ARTREA CIVIL PARISH

County:	Londonderry and Tyrone
Barony:	Loughinsholin in County Derry
	Dungannon Upper in County Tyrone
Diocese:	Armagh
Poor Law Union:	Magherafelt in County Derry
	Cookstown in County Tyrone
Probate District:	Londonderry in County Derry
	Armagh in County Tyrone
Area:	18,616 acres in County Derry (of which 2,071 acres is Lough Neagh)
	2,283 acres in County Tyrone
Population in 1831:	12,390
Topography:	Bounded in the northeast by Lough Neagh this parish is intersected by the Ballinderry River.
Towns:	Moneymore (population 1,025 in 1831)
Landowners in 1837:	The Drapers' Company and Salters' Company

RECORD SOURCES

Tithe:	1829
Griffith's Valuation:	1859 (Derry), 1860 (Tyrone)
Census:	1663 (Hearth Rolls), 1740 (Protestant Householders), 1766 (Religious Census), 1796 (Flax Lists), 1831, 1901 and 1911.

CHURCH REGISTERS

Church of Ireland:	Baptisms, marriages and burials from 1811.
	Ballyeglish – Baptisms and burials from 1868.
	Woods Chapel (15 townlands separated from Artrea) –
	Baptisms from 1807, marriages and burials from 1808.
Presbyterian:	1st Moneymore – Baptisms from 1827
	2nd Moneymore – Baptisms from 1845 (united 1920)
Roman Catholic:	Moneymore – Baptisms 1832-1834, 1838-1843 & from 1854; Marriages 1830-1843 & from 1854
Moravian Chapel:	in Ballymaguigan townland

GRAVEYARDS AND TOWNLANDS WHERE FOUND IN 1860:

	Ballyeglish, Ballymaguigan, Derrygarve and Drumenagh (all in County Derry)
Church of Ireland:	Lisnamarrow (Derry) and Tullyraw (Tyrone)
Roman Catholic:	Moneymore (Derry)

TOP TEN SURNAMES IN 1860 (in descending order):

1 O'Neill; 2 Devlin; 3= Brown and Ferguson; 5= McVeagh and Mulholland; 7= Lennox, Waterson and Wilson; 10 Donnelly

BALLINDERRY CIVIL PARISH

County:	Londonderry and Tyrone
Barony:	Loughinsholin in County Derry
	Dungannon Upper in County Tyrone
Diocese:	Armagh
Poor Law Union:	Magherafelt in County Derry
	Cookstown in County Tyrone
Probate District:	Londonderry in County Derry
	Armagh in County Tyrone
Area:	5,907 acres in County Derry (of which 2,939 acres is Lough Neagh)
	2,268 acres in County Tyrone
Population in 1831:	3,163
Topography:	This fertile parish, situated in the valley of the Ballinderry River, on the northwest shore of Lough Neagh, lies 7 miles southeast of Moneymore
Landowners in 1837:	Salters' Company

RECORD SOURCES

Tithe:	1834
Griffith's Valuation:	1859
Census:	1663 (Hearth Rolls), 1740 (Protestant Householders), 1796 (Flax Lists), 1831, 1901 and 1911.

CHURCH REGISTERS

Church of Ireland:	Baptisms and marriages from 1802 and burials from 1803. Now joined with Tamlaght and Arboe
Roman Catholic:	Ballinderry – Baptisms 1826-1838 & from 1841; Marriages from 1827.
Methodist Meeting House:	in Ballinderry townland

GRAVEYARDS AND TOWNLANDS WHERE FOUND IN 1859:

	The Gort alias Eglish (Tyrone)
Methodist:	Ballinderry (Derry)
Roman Catholic:	Ballylifford (Derry)

TOP TEN SURNAMES IN 1859 (in descending order):

1 McGuigan; 2 Taylor; 3= McKee and Quinn; 5 Mellon; 6 McCusker; 7 Devlin; 8 McCartney; 9= Clarke, Madden and Scullion

BALLYAGHRAN CIVIL PARISH

County:	Londonderry
Barony:	Northeast Liberties of Coleraine
Diocese:	Church of Ireland Diocese of Connor
	Roman Catholic Diocese of Down and Connor
Poor Law Union:	Coleraine
Probate District:	Londonderry
Area:	3,894 acres
Population in 1831:	2,746
Topography:	Bounded in the west by the River Bann and in the north by the Atlantic Ocean this fertile parish lies 3 miles northwest of the town of Coleraine.
Towns:	Portstewart (population of 475 in 1831)
Landowners in 1837:	J Cromie was the principal landholder.

RECORD SOURCES

Tithe:	1829
Griffith's Valuation:	1859
Census:	1663 (Hearth Rolls), 1740 (Protestant Householders), 1796 (Flax Lists), 1831, 1901 and 1911.

CHURCH REGISTERS

Church of Ireland:	Agherton – Baptisms 1845-1856, 1859 and from 1873.
Presbyterian:	Portstewart – Baptisms from 1829
Roman Catholic:	Coleraine – Baptisms and marriages from 1848
Methodist:	Portstewart – Baptisms from 1831

GRAVEYARDS AND TOWNLANDS WHERE FOUND IN 1859:

Glebe

TOP TEN SURNAMES IN 1859 (in descending order):

1 Martin; 2= Brown and Doherty; 4 Ross; 5= Boyd, McKerrigan, Moore, Shaw and Smith; 10= Black, Finlay, Huston and Law

BALLYMONEY CIVIL PARISH

County:	Londonderry and Antrim
Barony:	Northeast Liberties of Coleraine, County Derry
	Kilconway and Upper Dunluce, County Antrim
Diocese:	Church of Ireland Diocese of Connor
	Roman Catholic Diocese of Down and Connor
Poor Law Union:	Ballymoney
Probate District:	Londonderry in County Derry
	Belfast in County Antrim
Area:	632 acres in County Derry
	753 acres in Kilconway Barony, County Antrim
	21,303 acres in Upper Dunluce Barony, County Antrim
Population in 1831:	11,579
Topography:	This fertile parish is bounded on the west by the River Bann.
Towns:	Ballymoney (population 2,222 in 1831)

RECORD SOURCES

Tithe:	1825
Griffith's Valuation:	1859 (Derry), 1861 (Antrim)
Census:	1740 (Protestant Householders), 1796 (Flax Lists), 1831 (Derry), 1851 (townland of Garryduff in County Antrim), 1901 and 1911.

CHURCH REGISTERS

Church of Ireland:	Baptisms, marriages and burials from 1807. Now joined with Finvoy and Rasharkin
Presbyterian:	1st Ballymoney from 1751, 2nd Ballymoney or Trinity from 1845, 3rd Ballymoney or St James' from 1825, Roseyards from 1845, Drumreagh from 1864 and Garryduff
Roman Catholic:	Ballymoney and Derrykeighan - Baptisms and marriages from 1853
Methodist:	Ballymoney – Baptisms from 1831
Covenanter:	At Charlotte Street, Ballymoney in 1861
Unitarian:	At Charles Street, Ballymoney in 1861

GRAVEYARDS AND TOWNLANDS WHERE FOUND IN 1861:

Church of Ireland:	Church Street, Ballymoney
Presbyterian:	Drumreagh
Roman Catholic:	Castle Street, Ballymoney
Covenanter:	Charlotte Street, Ballymoney

TOP TEN SURNAMES IN 1861 (in descending order):

1 McLoughlin; 2= Boyd, Campbell and Thompson; 5= Stewart and Wilson; 7 Murphy; 8= Anderson, Doherty, Patterson and Robinson

BALLYNASCREEN CIVIL PARISH

County:	Londonderry
Barony:	Loughinsholin
Diocese:	Derry
Poor Law Union:	Magherafelt
Probate District:	Londonderry

Area:	32,520 acres
Population in 1831:	7,854
Topography:	Situated in the valley of the Moyola River this parish is bounded by the Sperrin Mountains to the west and by Slieve Gallion (1,623 feet) in the south.
Towns:	Draperstown (population 412 in 1831). To 1812 its name was Cross
Landowners in 1837:	The Drapers' Company, representatives of the Skinners' Company and the See of Derry

RECORD SOURCES

Tithe:	1825
Griffith's Valuation:	1859
Census:	1663 (Hearth Rolls), 1740 (Protestant Householders), 1766 (Religious Census), 1796 (Flax Lists), 1831, 1901 and 1911.

CHURCH REGISTERS

Church of Ireland:	Baptisms from 1808; marriages 1825-1826 and from 1828 and burials from 1824. Now joined with Kilcronaghan. Sixtowns – pre-1870 none. Now joined with Kilcronaghan
Presbyterian:	Draperstown - Baptisms and marriages from 1837.
Roman Catholic:	Draperstown – Baptisms 1836 and from 1846; marriages from 1834 and burials 1882-1884

GRAVEYARDS AND TOWNLANDS WHERE FOUND IN 1859:

	Moneyconey
Church of Ireland:	Cavanreagh and Moykeeran
Roman Catholic:	Straw

TOP TEN SURNAMES IN 1859 (in descending order):

1 Bradley; 2 Kelly; 3 Henry; 4 McWilliams; 5 Hagan; 6 McNamee; 7 Murray; 8 McGuiggan; 9= McGlade and McCloskey

BALLYRASHANE CIVIL PARISH

County:	Londonderry and Antrim
Barony:	Northeast Liberties of Coleraine in County Derry
	Lower Dunluce in County Antrim
Diocese:	Church of Ireland Diocese of Connor
	Roman Catholic Diocese of Down and Connor
Poor Law Union:	Coleraine in County Derry
	Ballymoney in County Antrim
Probate District:	Londonderry in County Derry
	Belfast in County Antrim
Area:	3,656 acres in County Derry
	2,689 acres in County Antrim
Population in 1831:	2,851
Topography:	This fertile parish is three miles northeast of the town of Coleraine.

RECORD SOURCES

Tithe:	1832
Griffith's Valuation:	1859 (Derry), 1861 (Antrim)
Census:	1740 (Protestant Householders), 1796 (Flax Lists), 1831, 1901 and 1911.

CHURCH REGISTERS

Church of Ireland:	Pre-1870 none. Now joined with Kildollagh.
Presbyterian:	Ballyrashane – Baptisms from 1863
	Ballywatt (or 2nd Ballyrashane) – Baptisms from 1867
Roman Catholic:	Portrush and Bushmills – Baptisms from 1844 and marriages from 1848

GRAVEYARDS AND TOWNLANDS WHERE FOUND IN 1861:

Church of Ireland:	Glebe (Derry)

TOP TEN SURNAMES IN 1861 (in descending order):

1 Sterling; 2 Anderson; 3= Acheson and Wilson; 5= Campbell, McDonnell, McMullen, Moore, Norris and Smith

BALLYSCULLION CIVIL PARISH

County:	Londonderry and Antrim
Barony:	Loughinsholin in County Derry
	Upper Toome in County Antrim
Diocese:	Derry
Poor Law Union:	Magherafelt in County Derry
	Ballymena in County Antrim
Probate District:	Londonderry in County Derry
	Belfast in County Antrim
Area:	11,035 acres in County Derry
	2,132 acres in County Antrim (of which 1,203 acres is Lough Beg)
Population in 1831:	6,543
Topography:	This parish of fertile lands and extensive bogs, divided by the River Bann, lies nine miles south of the town of Kilrea.
Towns:	Bellaghy
	Part of town of Castledawson (see Magherafelt)
Landowners in 1837:	Vintners' Company

RECORD SOURCES

Tithe:	1828
Griffith's Valuation:	1859 (Derry), 1862 (Antrim)
Census:	1663 (Hearth Rolls), 1740 (Protestant Householders), 1766 (Religious Census), 1796 (Flax Lists), 1831, 1901 and 1911.

CHURCH REGISTERS

Church of Ireland:	Baptisms from 1863.
Presbyterian:	Bellaghy (from 1836 to 1850 there was a second congregation, known as 2nd Bellaghy) – Baptisms from 1862.
Roman Catholic:	Bellaghy - Baptisms and marriages from 1844

GRAVEYARDS AND TOWNLANDS WHERE FOUND IN 1862:

	Church Island
Church of Ireland:	Church Lane, Bellaghy
Roman Catholic:	Tamlaghtduff

TOP TEN SURNAMES IN 1862 (in descending order):

1 Scullion; 2= Dimond and O'Neill; 4 McErlane; 5 Kennedy; 6 Cassidy; 7= Davidson and McQuillan; 9 McIntyre; 10 Kelly

BALLYWILLIN CIVIL PARISH

County:	Londonderry and Antrim
Barony:	Northeast Liberties of Coleraine in County Derry
	Lower Dunluce in County Antrim
Diocese:	Church of Ireland Diocese of Connor
	Roman Catholic Diocese of Down and Connor
Poor Law Union:	Coleraine
Probate District:	Londonderry in County Derry
	Belfast in County Antrim
Area:	3,056 acres in County Derry
	1,616 acres in County Antrim (including 24 acres of Skerry Islands)
Population in 1831:	2,219
Topography:	Bounded on the north by the Atlantic Ocean this largely fertile parish lies three miles northeast of the town of Coleraine.
Towns:	Portrush, County Antrim (population of 337 in 1831)

RECORD SOURCES

Tithe:	1831
Griffith's Valuation:	1859 (Derry), 1861 (Antrim)
Census:	1663 (Hearth Rolls), 1740 (Protestant Householders), 1796 (Flax Lists), 1831, 1901 and 1911.

CHURCH REGISTERS

Church of Ireland:	Ballywillan (Portrush) – Baptisms from 1826; marriages from 1825 and burials from 1827.
Presbyterian:	Ballywillan – Baptisms from 1862
	Portrush – Baptisms from 1843
Roman Catholic:	Portrush and Bushmills – Baptisms from 1844 and marriages from 1848
Methodist:	Portrush – Baptisms from 1831

GRAVEYARDS AND TOWNLANDS WHERE FOUND IN 1861:

Glebe

TOP TEN SURNAMES IN 1861 (in descending order):

1 Douglas; 2= Knox and Reid; 4 Stewart; 5 Black; 6= Campbell, Clarke, Kelly, McNeill and Rankin

BALTEAGH CIVIL PARISH

County:	Londonderry
Barony:	Keenaght
Diocese:	Derry
Poor Law Union:	NewtownLimavady
Probate District:	Londonderry
Area:	10,408 acres
Population in 1831:	3,326
Topography:	Bounded on the west by the River Roe and to the east by Keady Mountain (1,101 feet) this parish lies two miles southeast of the town of Limavady.
Landowners in 1837:	Except for a small portion belonging to the See of Derry this parish was chiefly the property of the Marquis of Waterford who acquired it from the Haberdashers' Company.

RECORD SOURCES

Tithe:	1829
Griffith's Valuation:	1858
Census:	1663 (Hearth Rolls), 1740 (Protestant Householders), 1796 (Flax Lists), 1831, 1901 and 1911.

CHURCH REGISTERS

Church of Ireland:	Pre-1870 none. Now joined with Carrick
Presbyterian:	Balteagh – Baptisms from 1868 (united with Bovevagh in 1975)
Roman Catholic:	Limavady – Baptisms begin 1855; Marriages from 1856 and Burials 1859-1869

GRAVEYARDS AND TOWNLANDS WHERE FOUND IN 1858:

Church of Ireland:	Ardmore
Presbyterian:	Lislane

TOP TEN SURNAMES IN 1858 (in descending order):

1= Mullen and Ross; 3 Kane; 4 Connor; 5= Doherty, Loughrey, McLoughlin and Oliver; 9 Quigg; 10= Anderson, Gault and Irwin

BANAGHER CIVIL PARISH

County:	Londonderry
Barony:	Tirkeeran and Keenaght
Diocese:	Derry
Poor Law Union:	Londonderry and NewtownLimavady
Probate District:	Londonderry
Area:	23,905 acres
Population in 1831:	4,086
Topograph	This mountainous parish in the heart of the Sperrin Mountains lies two miles southwest of the town of Dungiven.
Villages:	Feeny
Landowners in 1837:	Fishmongers' Company, Skinners' Company and the See of Derry.

RECORD SOURCES

Tithe:	1826
Griffith's Valuation:	1858
Census:	1663 (Hearth Rolls), 1740 (Protestant Householders), 1766 (Religious Census), 1796 (Flax Lists), 1831, 1901 and 1911.

CHURCH REGISTERS

Church of Ireland:	Baptisms from 1821; marriages from 1827 and burials from 1837. Now joined with Cumber Lower and Upper.
Presbyterian:	Banagher – Baptisms from 1834
Roman Catholic:	Feeny – Baptisms from 1848 and marriages from 1850.

GRAVEYARDS AND TOWNLANDS WHERE FOUND IN 1858:

	Magheramore
Church of Ireland:	Rallagh
Roman Catholic:	Fincarn

TOP TEN SURNAMES IN 1858 (in descending order):

1 McCluskey; 2 Hassan; 3 Kane; 4= Heaney and Mullen; 6 McFarlane; 7 Miller; 8= Craig and Thompson; 10= Murphy, O'Neill and Witherow

BOVEVAGH CIVIL PARISH

County:	Londonderry
Barony:	Keenaght
Diocese:	Derry
Poor Law Union:	NewtownLimavady
Probate District:	Londonderry
Area:	18,005 acres
Population in 1831:	5,552
Topography:	This fertile parish in the valley of the River Roe lies two miles north of the town of Dungiven.
Landowners in 1837:	The land to the east of the River Roe belonged to the Haberdashers' Company.

RECORD SOURCES

Tithe:	1827
Griffith's Valuation:	1859
Census:	1663 (Hearth Rolls), 1740 (Protestant Householders), 1766 (Religious Census), 1796 (Flax Lists), 1831, 1901 and 1911.

CHURCH REGISTERS

Church of Ireland:	Pre-1870 none. Now joined with Dungiven
Presbyterian:	Bovevagh – Baptisms 1818-1839 and from 1843; Marriages 1818-1830, 1834-1838 and from 1843 and burials 1870-1873 (united with Balteagh in 1975).
Roman Catholic:	Part Feeny – Baptisms from 1848 and marriages from 1850. Part Limavady – Baptisms begin 1855; Marriages from 1856 and Burials 1859-1869

GRAVEYARDS AND TOWNLANDS WHERE FOUND IN 1859:

Church of Ireland:	Bovevagh
Presbyterian:	Bovevagh
Roman Catholic:	Camnish
	Ballymoney

TOP TEN SURNAMES IN 1859 (in descending order):

1 McCloskey; 2 Mullen; 3 McLoughlin; 4 Brolly; 5= Carton and Kane; 7 Douglas; 8= Ferguson and McFadden; 10 Moore

CARRICK CIVIL PARISH

County:	Londonderry
Barony:	Keenaght
Diocese:	Derry
Poor Law Union:	NewtownLimavady
Probate District:	Londonderry
Area:	5,337 acres
Topography:	Bounded in the east by the River Roe this parish lies three miles south of the town of Limavady.
Landowners:	Much of the land was originally granted to Sir Thomas Phillips in the reign of James I.

RECORD SOURCES

Tithe: This parish was created in 1846 by separating 3 townlands from Balteagh Parish (Ballyquin, Carrick East and Maine South); 3 townlands from Bovevagh (Carrick, Mulkeeragh and Templemoyle); and 5 from Tamlaght Finlagan (Ballydarrog, Ballymore, Largy, Moys and Terrydrum). The relevant tithe entries will be found in these three parishes.

Griffith's Valuation: 1858

Census: 1663 (Hearth Rolls), 1740 (Protestant Householders), 1796 (Flax Lists) and 1831 – search Balteagh, Bovevagh or Tamlaght Finlagan Parishes. 1901 and 1911

CHURCH REGISTERS

Church of Ireland: Balteagh, Bovevagh or Tamlaght Finlagan for early entries. Carrick - Pre-1870 none. Now joined with Balteagh.
Presbyterian: Largy – Baptisms from 1848
Roman Catholic: Limavady – Baptisms begin 1855; Marriages from 1856 and Burials 1859-1869
Independent: At Ballydarrog in 1858

GRAVEYARDS AND TOWNLANDS WHERE FOUND IN 1858:

Presbyterian: Largy

TOP TEN SURNAMES IN 1858 (in descending order):

1 Smith; 2 McLoughlin; 3 Irwin; 4= Douglas, Fleming, McCloskey, Miller, Moore and Wallace; 10= Cassidy, Dunsheath, Ferguson, McClean, McClelland, Mullen, Purcell and Scott

CLONDERMOT CIVIL PARISH

County:	Londonderry
Barony:	Tirkeeran
Diocese:	Derry
Poor Law Union:	Londonderry
Probate District:	Londonderry
Area:	21,606 acres
Population in 1831:	10,388
Topography:	This parish is separated from the city of Londonderry by the River Foyle. The northern portion of the parish is fertile while the southern portion is mostly moorland.
Towns:	Waterside, a suburb of the city of Londondery
Landowners in 1837:	Goldsmiths' Company and Grocers' Company

RECORD SOURCES

Tithe:	1834
Griffith's Valuation:	1858
Census:	1663 (Hearth Rolls), 1740 (Protestant Householders), 1796 (Flax Lists), 1831, 1901 and 1911.

CHURCH REGISTERS

Church of Ireland:	Glendermott – Baptisms from 1810; marriages from 1808 and burials from 1828.
	Clooney – Baptisms and burials from 1867
Presbyterian:	Glendermott – Baptisms from 1855 (1st and 2nd Glendermott united in 1910)
	Gortnessy – Baptisms from 1839 (united with Faughanvale in 1977)
Roman Catholic:	Waterside (Glendermott) – Baptisms and marriages from 1864.
Reformed Presbyterian:	Bond's Hill, Londonderry
	Faughan – no pre-1900 baptisms

GRAVEYARDS AND TOWNLANDS WHERE FOUND IN 1858:

	Ballyshasky, Clondermot and Templetown
Church of Ireland:	Altnagelvin
Presbyterian:	Gortnessy
Roman Catholic:	Currynierin

TOP TEN SURNAMES IN 1858 (in descending order):

1 Doherty; 2 Smith; 3 McLaughlin; 4 Lynch; 5 McCafferty; 6 Donaghy; 7= Kelly, Logue, Mitchell, Thompson and Wilson

COLERAINE CIVIL PARISH

County:	Londonderry
Barony:	Northeast Liberties of Coleraine
Diocese:	Church of Ireland Diocese of Connor
	Roman Catholic Diocese of Down and Connor
Poor Law Union:	Coleraine
Probate District:	Londonderry
Area:	4,860 acres
Population in 1831:	7,646
Topography:	This fertile parish is bounded on the west by the River Bann.
Towns:	Coleraine (population of 5,668 in 1831)
Landowners in 1837:	The Irish Society

RECORD SOURCES

Tithe:	1827
Griffith's Valuation:	1859
Census:	1663 (Hearth Rolls), 1740 (Protestant Householders), 1796 (Flax Lists), 1831, 1901 and 1911.

CHURCH REGISTERS

Church of Ireland:	Baptisms, marriages and burials from 1769
Presbyterian:	1st Coleraine – Baptisms from 1845
	2nd Coleraine (New Row) – Baptisms from 1842 and marriages from 1809
	3rd Coleraine (Terrace Row) – Baptisms from 1862
Roman Catholic:	Coleraine – Baptisms and marriages from 1848
Methodist:	Coleraine – Baptisms from 1831
Congregational:	Coleraine – Baptisms from 1837
Baptist:	at Meeting House Place, Coleraine in 1859

GRAVEYARDS AND TOWNLANDS WHERE FOUND IN 1859:

Church of Ireland:	Church Street, Coleraine

TOP TEN SURNAMES IN 1859 (in descending order):

1 Kane; 2 Doherty; 3 Kennedy; 4 Mullen; 5 Black; 6= Boyd, Clarke, Glenn, McCormick, McGonigle, McLoughlin and Wilson

CUMBER LOWER CIVIL PARISH

County:	Londonderry
Barony:	Tirkeeran
Diocese:	Derry
Poor Law Union:	Londonderry
Probate District:	Londonderry
Area:	14,466 acres
Population in 1831:	4,584
Topography:	This fertile parish in the valley of the River Faughan lies six miles southeast of the city of Londonderry. This parish was separated from the original parish of Cumber in 1794.
Landowners in 1837:	Goldsmiths' Company, Grocers' Company and Skinners' Company.

RECORD SOURCES

Tithe:	1827
Griffith's Valuation:	1858
Census:	1663 (Hearth Rolls), 1740 (Protestant Householders), (1766 Religious Census – merely a numerical count of Protestants and Roman Catholics by townland), 1796 (Flax Lists), 1831, 1901 and 1911.

CHURCH REGISTERS

Church of Ireland:	Baptisms from 1804; marriages from 1806 and burials 1825 and from 1855. Now joined with Banagher, Cumber Upper and Learmount.
Presbyterian:	Cumber Lower – Baptisms from 1827 and marriages from 1843 (united with Cumber Upper in 1976)
Roman Catholic:	Faughanvale – Baptisms from 1863 and marriages from 1863.

GRAVEYARDS AND TOWNLANDS WHERE FOUND IN 1858:

Church of Ireland:	Killaloo
Roman Catholic:	Mullaboy

TOP TEN SURNAMES IN 1858 (in descending order):

1 McLoughlin; 2 Miller; 3 McGuinness; 4= Brown, Campbell, Feeny and Kelly; 8= Quigley, Simpson and Thompson

CUMBER UPPER CIVIL PARISH

County:	Londonderry
Barony:	Tirkeeran
Diocese:	Derry
Poor Law Union:	Londonderry and NewtownLimavady
Probate District:	Londonderry
Area:	17,597 acres
Population in 1831:	5,430
Topography:	Mountainous in the southern parts this parish lies seven miles southeast of the city of Londonderry. This parish was separated from the original parish of Cumber in 1794.
Villages:	Claudy (population of 180 in 1831)
Landowners in 1837:	Fishmongers' Company and Skinners' Company.

RECORD SOURCES

Tithe:	1828
Griffith's Valuation:	1858
Census:	1663 (Hearth Rolls), 1740 (Protestant Householders), (1766 Religious Census – merely a numerical count of Protestants and Roman Catholics by townland), 1796 (Flax Lists), 1831, 1901 and 1911.

CHURCH REGISTERS

Church of Ireland:	Baptisms 1811-1818 and from 1826; marriages 1811-1814 and from 1826 and burials from 1837. Now joined with Banagher, Cumber Upper and Learmount.
Presbyterian:	Cumber Upper – Baptisms and marriages from 1834 (united with Cumber Lower in 1976)
Roman Catholic:	Claudy – Baptisms 1853-1854 and from 1863 and marriages from 1863.

GRAVEYARDS AND TOWNLANDS WHERE FOUND IN 1858:

Church of Ireland:	Cumber
Roman Catholic:	Village of Claudy

TOP TEN SURNAMES IN 1858 (in descending order):

1 Devine; 2 McCluskey; 3= McDonagh and Mullen; 5 Hamilton; 6 Hassan; 7= Christie, Doherty, McLoughlin and Rosborough

DERRYLORAN CIVIL PARISH

County:	Londonderry and Tyrone
Barony:	Loughinsholin in County Derry
	Dungannon Upper in County Tyrone
Diocese:	Armagh
Poor Law Union:	Magherafelt in County Derry
	Cookstown in County Tyrone
Probate District:	Londonderry in County Derry
	Armagh in County Tyrone
Area:	2,444 acres in County Derry
	9,556 acres in County Tyrone
Population in 1831:	8,406
Topography:	A fertile parish, in the valley of the Ballinderry River, situated between the Sperrin Mountains and Lough Neagh.
Towns:	Cookstown (population of 2,883 in 1831)
Landowners in 1837:	Drapers' Company were the chief landlords

RECORD SOURCES

Tithe:	1826
Griffith's Valuation:	1859 (Derry), 1860 (Tyrone)
Census:	1663 (Hearth Rolls), 1740 (Protestant Householders), 1766 (Religious Census), 1796 (Flax Lists), 1831, 1901 and 1911.

CHURCH REGISTERS

Church of Ireland:	Baptisms and marriages from 1797 and burials from 1795.
Presbyterian:	1st Cookstown – Baptisms from 1836
	2nd and 3rd Cookstown (united in 1929 and now known as Molesworth Street)
	Sandholes – Baptisms from 1844
Roman Catholic:	Cookstown – Baptisms and marriages from 1827
Methodist:	Cookstown
Baptist:	Cookstown

GRAVEYARDS AND TOWNLANDS WHERE FOUND IN 1860:

	Glebe and Tullagh (Tyrone)
Roman Catholic:	Gortalowry (Tyrone)

TOP TEN SURNAMES IN 1860 (in descending order):

1 Mullen; 2 Quinn; 3 Bell; 4 Miller; 5= Devlin and Glasgow; 7 Johnson; 8= Allen and Hamilton; 10 Henry

DESERTLYN CIVIL PARISH

County:	Londonderry
Barony:	Loughinsholin
Diocese:	Armagh
Poor Law Union:	Magherafelt
Probate District:	Londonderry

Area:	5,561 acres
Population in 1831:	3,318
Topography:	Situated in a valley of the Ballinderry River this parish is bounded in the west by Slieve Gallion (1,623 feet).
Towns:	Part of Moneymore (see Artrea)

RECORD SOURCES

Tithe:	1828
Griffith's Valuation:	1859
Census:	1663 (Hearth Rolls), 1740 (Protestant Householders), 1766 (Religious Census), 1796 (Flax Lists), 1831, 1901 and 1911.

CHURCH REGISTERS

Church of Ireland:	Baptisms and marriages from 1797 and burials from 1798. Now joined with Ballyeglish.
Roman Catholic:	Moneymore – Baptisms 1832-1834, 1838-1843 and from 1854; marriages 1830-1843 and from 1854.
Methodist:	Moneymore
Baptist:	at townland of Carndaisy in 1859

GRAVEYARDS AND TOWNLANDS WHERE FOUND IN 1859:

	Ballymully and Lawford Street, Moneymore
Church of Ireland:	Smith Street, Moneymore

TOP TEN SURNAMES IN 1859 (in descending order):

1 Stewart; 2 Devlin; 3 Wright; 4 Anderson; 5 Richey; 6= Cousley, Muldoon and Smith; 9= Allen, Brown, Campbell, Crookes, Farley, Maxwell, Rea, Shannon and Wilson

DESERTMARTIN CIVIL PARISH

County:	Londonderry
Barony:	Loughinsholin
Diocese:	Derry
Poor Law Union:	Magherafelt
Probate District:	Londonderry
Area:	9,579 acres
Population in 1831:	4,934
Topography:	This fertile parish in the valley of the Moyola River is bounded by Slieve Gallion (1,623 feet) in the southwest. It lies two miles west of the town of Magherafelt.
Villages:	Desertmartin (population of 257 in 1831)
Landowners in 1837:	The Drapers' Company was the chief proprietor. Small portions were also owned by the Vintners' and Salters' Companies.

RECORD SOURCES

Tithe:	1827
Griffith's Valuation:	1859
Census:	1663 (Hearth Rolls), 1740 (Protestant Householders), 1766 (Religious Census), 1796 (Flax Lists), 1831, 1901 and 1911.

CHURCH REGISTERS

Church of Ireland:	Baptisms from 1785; marriages from 1784 and burials 1783, 1788, 1829 and from 1842. Now joined with Termoneeny.
Presbyterian:	Lecumpher – Baptisms and marriages from 1825 (united with Union Road, Magherafelt in 1926)
Roman Catholic:	Desertmartin – Baptisms, marriages and burials from 1848

GRAVEYARDS AND TOWNLANDS WHERE FOUND IN 1859:

	Annagh and Moneysterlin, and Desertmartin
Church of Ireland:	Dromore
Roman Catholic:	Cullion and Desertmartin

TOP TEN SURNAMES IN 1859 (in descending order):

1 McGuckin; 2= O'Neill and Walls; 4 McGovern; 5= Bradley and McWilliams; 7 Johnston; 8= Henry, Laycock and McCrystal

DESERTOGHILL CIVIL PARISH

County:	Londonderry
Barony:	Coleraine
Diocese:	Derry
Poor Law Union:	Ballymoney & Coleraine
Probate District:	Londonderry
Area:	11,466 acres
Population in 1831:	4,701
Topography:	This parish, which lies one mile southeast of the town of Garvagh, is situated in the foothills between the Bann Valley and the mountains of north Derry.
Landowners in 1837:	The Ironmongers' Company and Mercers' Company.

RECORD SOURCES

Tithe:	1832
Griffith's Valuation:	1859
Census:	1663 (Hearth Rolls), 1740 (Protestant Householders), 1796 (Flax Lists), 1831, 1901 and 1911.

CHURCH REGISTERS

Church of Ireland:	Pre-1870 none. Now joined with Errigal
Presbyterian:	Moneydig - Baptisms from 1857
Roman Catholic:	Kilrea – Baptisms, marriages and burials from 1846.

GRAVEYARDS AND TOWNLANDS WHERE FOUND IN 1859:

	Ballynameen
Church of Ireland:	Moyletra Kill
Presbyterian:	Moneydig

TOP TEN SURNAMES IN 1859 (in descending order):

1= Bradley, Kane and Stewart; 4 Campbell; 5 Torrens; 6 Holmes; 7 Dimond; 8= Boyd and Gilmore; 10 Morell

DRUMACHOSE CIVIL PARISH

County:	Londonderry
Barony:	Keenaght
Diocese:	Derry
Poor Law Union:	NewtownLimavady
Probate District:	Londonderry

Area:	11,682 acres
Population in 1831:	5,280
Topography:	Bounded by the River Roe in the west and by the mountains of north Derry, including Keady Mountain (1,101 feet), in the east.
Towns;	NewtownLimavady (known today as Limavady – population of 2,428 in 1831)
Landowners in 1837:	The western portion (including the town of Limavady), which was originally granted to Sir Thomas Phillips by James I, belonged to the freehold estate of NewtownLimavady while the Haberdashers' Company owned the eastern part. A small portion was also owned by the See of Derry.

RECORD SOURCES

Tithe:	1826
Griffith's Valuation:	1858
Census:	1663 (Hearth Rolls), 1740 (Protestant Householders), 1766 (Religious Census), 1796 (Flax Lists), 1831, 1901 and 1911.

CHURCH REGISTERS

Church of Ireland:	Baptisms from 1729 (with gaps); marriages from 1728 (with gaps) and burials from 1730 (with gaps)
Presbyterian:	Derramore – Baptisms from 1825
	Drumachose – Baptisms from 1837
	1st Limavady – Baptisms 1832-1839 and from 1861; marriages 1832-1841
	2nd Limavady
Roman Catholic:	Limavady – Baptisms from 1855; marriages from 1856 and burials 1859-1869
Methodist:	Limavady – Baptisms from 1841
Reformed Presbyterian:	Limavady
Congregational:	Limavady
Independent:	at Irish Green Street, Limavady in 1858
Unitarian:	at Meeting House Lane, Limavady in 1858

GRAVEYARDS AND TOWNLANDS WHERE FOUND IN 1858:

	Coolessan and Drummond
Church of Ireland:	Main Street, Limavady
Presbyterian:	Rathbrady More

TOP TEN SURNAMES IN 1858 (in descending order):
1 McLaughlin; 2 Mullen; 3 Kane; 4 Smith; 5 Stewart; 6 Doherty; 7= Connor and Moore; 9= Campbell, Douglas and Ferguson

DUNBOE CIVIL PARISH

County:	Londonderry
Barony:	Coleraine
Diocese:	Derry
Poor Law Union:	Coleraine
Probate District:	Londonderry
Area:	10,577 acres
Population in 1831:	5,018
Topography:	Bounded on the north by the Atlantic Ocean, on the west by the mountains of Binevenagh (1,260 feet) and to the east by the River Bann this parish lies five miles west of the town of Coleraine.
Villages:	Articlave
Landowners in 1837:	This parish partly belonged to Sir James R Bruce (of Downhill) and partly to the Clothworkers' Company

RECORD SOURCES

Tithe:	1828
Griffith's Valuation:	1859
Census:	1663 (Hearth Rolls), 1740 (Protestant Householders), 1796 (Flax Lists), 1831, 1901 and 1911.

CHURCH REGISTERS

Church of Ireland:	Castlerock – Pre-1870 none.
	Dunboe – Baptisms from 1839 and marriages and burials from 1845. Castlerock, Dunboe and Fermoyle is now a united parish.
Presbyterian:	Castlerock – Baptisms from 1875
	1st Dunboe – Baptisms 1805-1812, 1825-1826 and from 1843
Roman Catholic:	Coleraine – Baptisms from 1843

GRAVEYARDS AND TOWNLANDS WHERE FOUND IN 1859:

Church of Ireland:	Village of Articlave
Presbyterian:	Village of Articlave

TOP TEN SURNAMES IN 1859 (in descending order):

1= Doherty and Wark; 3 Mullen; 4= Blair and Smith; 6 Lees; 7= Hyndman and Thompson; 9= Kennedy and Tosh

DUNGIVEN CIVIL PARISH

County:	Londonderry
Barony:	Keenaght
Diocese:	Derry
Poor Law Union:	NewtownLimavady
Probate District:	Londonderry
Area:	29,298 acres
Population in 1831:	3,565
Topography:	Situated in the Roe Valley this parish is bounded by the Sperrin Mountains to the south and by the mountains of Benbradagh (1,535 feet) to the east. This parish was the seat of the O'Cahans (O'Kane).
Towns:	Dungiven (population of 1,162 in 1831)
Landowners in 1837:	The chief property holder was Robert Ogilby (of Pellipar House) who held it by lease from the Skinners' Company. A small portion in the north of the parish was held by the Haberdashers' Company.

RECORD SOURCES

Tithe:	1833
Griffith's Valuation:	1859
Census:	1663 (Hearth Rolls), 1740 (Protestant Householders), 1766 (Religious Census), 1796 (Flax Lists), 1831, 1901 and 1911.

CHURCH REGISTERS

Church of Ireland:	Baptisms from 1795; marriages 1795-1826 and from 1828 and burials from 1824. Now joined with Bovevagh.
Presbyterian:	Dungiven – Baptisms from 1836 and marriages from 1837. 1st and 2nd Dungiven united in 1849 Scriggan – Dissolved in 1905.
Roman Catholic:	Dungiven – Baptisms 1825-1834 and from 1847; marriages 1825-1834 and from 1864; and burials 1825-1832 and 1870-1871.

GRAVEYARDS AND TOWNLANDS WHERE FOUND IN 1859:

	Dungiven
Church of Ireland:	Dungiven
Roman Catholic:	Gortgarn

TOP TEN SURNAMES IN 1859 (in descending order):

1 McCloskey; 2= Kane and Kealy; 4 Irwin; 5 McLoughlin; 6 Mullen; 7 Morrison; 8 Doherty; 9= Heney and Scott

ERRIGAL CIVIL PARISH

County:	Londonderry
Barony:	Coleraine
Diocese:	Derry
Poor Law Union:	Coleraine
Probate District:	Londonderry

Area:	19,625 acres
Population in 1831:	5,401
Topography:	Bounded by the Agivey River in the south and by the mountains of north Derry, including Donalds Hill (1,318 feet), on its western flank.
Towns:	Garvagh
Landowners in 1837:	The Merchant Taylors' Company in the northern portion and the Ironmongers' Company in the southern part.

RECORD SOURCES

Tithe:	1825
Griffith's Valuation:	1859
Census:	1663 (Hearth Rolls), 1740 (Protestant Householders), 1796 (Flax Lists), 1831, 1901 and 1911.

CHURCH REGISTERS

Church of Ireland:	Pre-1870 none. Now joined with Desertoghill
Presbyterian:	1st Garvagh - Baptisms 1795-1816, 1822-1849 and from 1859 and marriages 1795-1802, 1807-1814 and from 1822. Census of congregation 1796 and 1840. 2nd Garvagh (Main Street) – Baptisms and marriages from 1830 and burials from 1853. United with Killaig in 1977. 3rd Garvagh – Dissolved in 1908.
Roman Catholic:	Garvagh – Baptisms from 1846.

GRAVEYARDS AND TOWNLANDS WHERE FOUND IN 1859:

Church of Ireland:	Ballintemple Garvagh
Presbyterian:	Main Street (2nd), Garvagh and Meeting House Lane (1st), Garvagh

TOP TEN SURNAMES IN 1859 (in descending order):

1 Mullen; 2 O'Kane; 3 McNicholl; 4 McAlister; 5= Kelly, Moore and Young; 8 Stewart, 9= Doherty and McCluskey

FAUGHANVALE CIVIL PARISH

County:	Londonderry
Barony:	Tirkeeran
Diocese:	Derry
Poor Law Union:	Londonderry and NewtownLimavady
Probate District:	Londonderry
Area:	20,496 acres
Population in 1831:	6,218
Topography:	Bounded on the north by Lough Foyle this fertile parish lies eight miles southeast of the city of Londonderry.
Villages:	Faughanvale and Muff (renamed Eglinton in 1858)
Landowners in 1837:	Grocers' Company and Fishmongers' Company

RECORD SOURCES

Tithe:	1835
Griffith's Valuation:	1858
Census:	1663 (Hearth Rolls), 1740 (Protestant Householders), 1796 (Flax Lists), 1803 (Private Census by Rev Ellis Thackeray), 1831, 1901 and 1911.

CHURCH REGISTERS

Church of Ireland:	Baptisms, marriages and burials from 1802.
Presbyterian:	Faughanvale – Baptisms from 1819
Roman Catholic:	Faughanvale – Baptisms from 1863 and marriages from 1860.

GRAVEYARDS AND TOWNLANDS WHERE FOUND IN 1858:

Church of Ireland:	Faughanvale Muff

TOP TEN SURNAMES IN 1858 (in descending order):

1= Doherty and McLoughlin; 3 Mullen; 4 Donaghy; 5 Louge; 6= Craig, Duddy, Hara, Kane and McGuinness

FORMOYLE CIVIL PARISH

County:	Londonderry
Barony:	Coleraine
Diocese:	Derry
Poor Law Union:	Coleraine
Probate District:	Londonderry
Area:	4,271 acres
Topography:	Bounded on the west by the mountains of Binevenagh (1,260 feet) this parish lies six miles west of the town of Coleraine.
Landowners in 1837:	Clothworkers' Company

RECORD SOURCES

Tithe:	This parish was created in 1843 by separating 9 townlands from Dunboe Parish (Altibrian, Ballinrees, Ballystrone, Belgarrow, Bratwell, Formoyle, Formullen, Knockmult and Sconce). The relevant tithe entries will be found in the Dunboe book.
Griffith's Valuation:	1858
Census:	1663 (Hearth Rolls), 1740 (Protestant Householders), 1796 (Flax Lists) and 1831 Census entries will be found in Dunboe Parish. 1901 and 1911.

CHURCH REGISTERS

Church of Ireland:	Dunboe for early entries.
	Formoyle – Baptisms from 1860; marriages from 1844 and burials from 1864. Now joined with Castlerock and Dunboe.
Presbyterian:	2nd Dunboe – Baptisms 1835-1848, 1853, 1858 and from 1864; and marriages from 1835
Roman Catholic:	Coleraine – Baptisms from 1843

GRAVEYARDS AND TOWNLANDS WHERE FOUND IN 1858:

No graveyards recorded in 1858

TOP TEN SURNAMES IN 1858 (in descending order):

1 Cunning; 2= Blair and McClelland; 4= Allen, Bradley, Caldwell and Cameron; 8= Craig and McClement; 10= Caskey, Glynn, Millen and Ross

KILCRONAGHAN CIVIL PARISH

County: Londonderry
Barony: Loughinsholin
Diocese: Derry
Poor Law Union: Magherafelt
Probate District: Londonderry

Area: 7,979 acres
Population in 1831: 4,186
Topography: This fertile parish is situated in the valley of the Moyola River.
Towns: Tobermore (population of 679 in 1831)
Landowners in 1837: The Vintners' Company and Drapers' Company.

RECORD SOURCES

Tithe: 1828
Griffith's Valuation: 1859
Census: 1663 (Hearth Rolls), 1740 (Protestant Householders), 1796 (Flax Lists), 1831, 1901 and 1911.

CHURCH REGISTERS

Church of Ireland: Baptisms from 1790; marriages from 1748 and burials 1828-1829 and from 1831. Now joined with Draperstown and Sixtowns.
Presbyterian: Tobermore – Baptisms from 1860
Roman Catholic: Desertmartin – Baptisms, marriages and burials from 1848.
Baptist: at Main Street, Tobermore in 1859

GRAVEYARDS AND TOWNLANDS WHERE FOUND IN 1859:

	Mormeal
Presbyterian:	Main Street, Tobermore

TOP TEN SURNAMES IN 1859 (in descending order):

1 Kelly; 2 McGuiggan; 3 Nelson; 4 Treanor; 5 Henry; 6 Hagan; 7 Lyle; 8= Hughes, Johnson, O'Neill and Stewart

KILDOLLAGH CIVIL PARISH

County:	Londonderry and Antrim
Barony:	Northeast Liberties of Coleraine in County Derry
	Upper Dunluce in County Antrim
Diocese:	Church of Ireland Diocese of Connor
	Roman Catholic Diocese of Down and Connor
Poor Law Union:	Coleraine
Probate District:	Londonderry in County Derry
	Belfast in County Antrim
Area:	1,962 acres in County Derry
	22 acres in County Antrim
Population in 1831:	982
Topography:	Bounded on the west by the River Bann this fertile parish is two miles southeast of the town of Coleraine.

RECORD SOURCES

Tithe:	1834
Griffith's Valuation:	1858
Census:	1831, 1901 and 1911.

CHURCH REGISTERS

Church of Ireland:	Pre-1870 none. Now joined with Ballyrashane
Roman Catholic:	Coleraine – Baptisms and marriages from 1848

GRAVEYARDS AND TOWNLANDS WHERE FOUND IN 1858:

Church of Ireland: Fishloughan

TOP TEN SURNAMES IN 1858 (in descending order):

1 Morrison; 2 Wilson; 3= Freeman, Galbraith and Kirkpatrick; 6= Kennedy, McNaul and Watt; 9= Adams, Boyd, Campbell, Cox, Doherty, Moore, Nicholl, Reid, Semple, Smith and Wallace

KILLELAGH CIVIL PARISH

County: Londonderry
Barony: Loughinsholin
Diocese: Derry
Poor Law Union: Magherafelt
Probate District: Londonderry

Area: 13,303 acres
Population in 1831: 3,045
Topography: This parish which is bounded on its eastern boundary by Carntogher mountain (1,521 feet), and lies 2 miles north of the town of Maghera, was separated from Maghera parish in 1794.
Villages: Swatragh (population of 204 in 1831)
Landowners in 1837: The Mercers' Company, the Ironmongers' Company and the See of Derry.

RECORD SOURCES

Tithe: 1833
Griffith's Valuation: 1859
Census: 1663 (Hearth Rolls), 1740 (Protestant Householders), 1796 (Flax Lists), 1831, 1901 and 1911.

CHURCH REGISTERS

Church of Ireland: Pre-1870 none. Now joined with Maghera.
Presbyterian: Swatragh – Baptisms from 1851 (united with Culnady in 1898)
Roman Catholic: Maghera – Baptisms and marriages from 1841 and burials 1848-1888.
Swatragh established 1887.

GRAVEYARDS AND TOWNLANDS WHERE FOUND IN 1859:

Roman Catholic: Granaghan

TOP TEN SURNAMES IN 1859 (in descending order):

1 Bradley; 2 Convery; 3= Kane and McIldowney; 5= Doherty and Gribbin; 7= Dimond, Lytle and McShane; 10 Slamon

KILLOWEN CIVIL PARISH

County:	Londonderry
Barony:	Coleraine
Diocese:	Derry
Poor Law Union:	Coleraine
Probate District:	Londonderry
Area:	1,806 acres
Population in 1831:	2,906
Topography:	Forming part of the suburbs of the town of Coleraine this parish is situated on the west bank of the River Bann.
Towns:	Waterside, a suburb of the town of Coleraine
Landowners in 1837:	Clothworkers' Company who held it by lease from the Irish Society

RECORD SOURCES

Tithe:	1830
Griffith's Valuation:	1859
Census:	1663 (Hearth Rolls), 1740 (Protestant Householders), 1796 (Flax Lists), 1831, 1901 and 1911.

CHURCH REGISTERS

Church of Ireland:	Baptisms and marriages from 1824 and burials 1825-1830 and from 1843
Presbyterian:	Various unsuccessful attempts were made to establish a congregation at Killowen between 1842 and 1868
Roman Catholic:	Coleraine – Baptisms from 1843

GRAVEYARDS AND TOWNLANDS WHERE FOUND IN 1859:

Church of Ireland:	Killowen Street, Coleraine
Roman Catholic:	Churchland

TOP TEN SURNAMES IN 1859 (in descending order):

1 Miller; 2 Anderson; 3= Doherty, Gibson, Kane, Kerr and McLoughlin; 8= Andrews, Campbell, Curry, Henry and Smith

KILREA CIVIL PARISH

County:	Londonderry
Barony:	Part Coleraine and part Loughinsholin
Diocese:	Derry
Poor Law Union:	Ballymoney
Probate District:	Londonderry
Area:	6,313 acres
Population in 1831:	4,262
Topography:	This parish extends for six miles along the western banks of the River Bann.
Towns:	Kilrea (population of 973 in 1831)
Landowners in 1837:	The Mercers' Company

RECORD SOURCES

Tithe:	1826
Griffith's Valuation:	1858
Census:	1663 (Hearth Rolls), 1740 (Protestant Householders), 1796 (Flax Lists), 1831, 1901 and 1911.

CHURCH REGISTERS

Church of Ireland:	Baptisms from 1801; marriages 1802-1805 and from 1829 and burials 1802-1804 and from 1829. Now joined with Aghadowey.
Presbyterian:	1st Kilrea – Baptisms 1825-1859 and from 1862 and marriages from 1825 2nd Kilrea – Baptisms from 1840. United with Boveedy in 1923.
Roman Catholic:	Kilrea – Baptisms, marriages and burials from 1846.

GRAVEYARDS AND TOWNLANDS WHERE FOUND IN 1858:

Church of Ireland:	Church Street, Kilrea
Presbyterian:	Church Street (1st), Kilrea and Maghera Street (2nd), Kilrea.

TOP TEN SURNAMES IN 1858 (in descending order):

1 Bradley; 2 Dimond; 3= Darragh and Gordon; 5 McKay; 6 Henry; 7 Campbell; 8 Hegarty; 9 Hunter; 10= Irwin and McGregor

LEARMOUNT CIVIL PARISH

County:	Londonderry and Tyrone
Barony:	Tirkeeran in County Derry
	Strabane Lower in County Tyrone
Diocese:	Derry
Poor Law Union:	Londonderry in County Derry
	Gortin in County Tyrone
Probate District:	Londonderry
Area:	17,613 acres
Population in 1831:	4,411
Topography:	Bounded by Sawel Mountain, which rises to 2,236 feet, this fertile parish lies five miles west of the town of Dungiven.
Villages:	Park (also known as Learmount)
Landowners in 1837:	Barre Beresford

RECORD SOURCES

Tithe:	This parish was created in 1831 by separating 11 townlands from Banagher Parish (Altinure Lower, Altinure Upper, Clagan, Dreen, Eden, Kilcreen, Loughtilube, Moneyhoghan, Straid, Tamnagh and Terrydreen); and 8 from Cumber Upper (Ballyrory, Carnanbane, Carnanreagh, Gortscreagan, Kilgort, Lear, Teenaght and Tireighter). The townland of Stranagalwilly in Cumber Upper Parish, County Tyrone was also added to Learmount. The relevant tithe entries will be found in these two parishes.
Griffith's Valuation:	1858 (Derry), 1860 (Tyrone)
Census:	1663 (Hearth Rolls), 1740 (Protestant Householders), 1796 (Flax Lists) and 1831 Census entries will be found in either Banagher or Cumber Upper parish. 1901 and 1911.

CHURCH REGISTERS

Church of Ireland:	Banagher or Cumber Upper for early entries.
	Learmount – Baptisms and burials from 1832 and marriages from 1833. Now joined with Cumber Upper, Cumber Lower and Banagher.
Presbyterian:	Banagher – Baptisms from 1834
Roman Catholic:	Claudy (Cumber Upper & Learmount) – Baptisms 1853-1854 and from 1863 and marriages from 1863.

GRAVEYARDS AND TOWNLANDS WHERE FOUND IN 1860:

	Straid
Church of Ireland:	Tireighter
Roman Catholic:	Gortscreagan

TOP TEN SURNAMES IN 1860 (in descending order):

1 McLoughlin; 2= Keane and McDonagh; 4 McClusky; 5 Gormley; 6 Kirlin; 7 Devin; 8 Mullen; 9 Carton; 10 Feeny

LISSAN CIVIL PARISH

County:	Londonderry and Tyrone
Barony:	Loughinsholin in County Derry
	Dungannon Upper in County Tyrone
Diocese:	Armagh
Poor Law Union:	Magherafelt in County Derry
	Cookstown in County Tyrone
Probate District:	Londonderry in County Derry
	Armagh in County Tyrone
Area:	11,767 acres in County Derry
	12,917 acres in County Tyrone
Population in 1831:	6,163
Topography:	Situated in the valley of the Ballinderry River this parish which is bounded on the north by Slieve Gallion (1,623 feet) lies three miles to the northeast of the town of Cookstown.
Landowners in 1837:	The See of Armagh and the Drapers' Company were the chief landlords.

RECORD SOURCES

Tithe:	1827
Griffith's Valuation:	1859 (Derry), 1860 (Tyrone)
Census:	1663 (Hearth Rolls), 1740 (Protestant Householders), 1796 (Flax Lists), 1831, 1901 and 1911.

CHURCH REGISTERS

Church of Ireland:	Baptisms 1753-1795 and from 1804; marriages 1744-1793 and from 1817 and burials 1753-1795 and from 1803.
Presbyterian:	Claggan – Baptisms and marriages from 1848. United with Orritor in 1958.
Roman Catholic:	Lissan – Baptisms and marriages from 1839

GRAVEYARDS AND TOWNLANDS WHERE FOUND IN 1860:

No graveyards recorded in 1860.

TOP TEN SURNAMES IN 1860 (in descending order):

1 O'Neill; 2= Bell, McGlone and Mallon; 5= Conlan, Corr, Donnelly and Quinn; 9= Crooke and McCullagh

MACOSQUIN CIVIL PARISH

County:	Londonderry
Barony:	Coleraine
Diocese:	Derry
Poor Law Union:	Coleraine
Probate District:	Londonderry
Area:	17,812 acres
Population in 1831:	6,639
Topography:	This fertile parish, two miles southwest of the town of Coleraine, is bounded by the mountains of north Derry in the west and by the River Bann in the east.
Landowners in 1837:	This parish was chiefly owned by the Richardson family who had purchased it from the Merchant Taylors' Company. Small portions were also the property of the Clothworkers' and Ironmongers' Companies.

RECORD SOURCES

Tithe:	1830
Griffith's Valuation:	1859
Census:	1663 (Hearth Rolls), 1740 (Protestant Householders), 1796 (Flax Lists), 1831, 1901 and 1911.

CHURCH REGISTERS

Church of Ireland:	Camus-Juxta-Bann (Macosquin) - Pre-1870 none.
Presbyterian:	Crossgar - Baptisms from 1839. United with Aghadowey in 1970.
	Dromore – United with Drumreagh in 1973.
	Macosquin – Baptisms 1823-1845, 1860 and from 1867.
Roman Catholic:	Coleraine – Baptisms from 1843
Reformed Presbyterian;	Ballylagan

GRAVEYARDS AND TOWNLANDS WHERE FOUND IN 1859:

	Camus
Presbyterian:	Crossgar
Reformed Presbyterian:	Ballylagan

TOP TEN SURNAMES IN 1859 (in descending order):

1= Black and Kennedy; 3 Moore; 4= Campbell and Smith; 6 Bennett; 7 Henry; 8= Blake, McLoughlin and Tannahill

MAGHERA CIVIL PARISH

County:	Londonderry
Barony:	Loughinsholin
Diocese:	Derry
Poor Law Union:	Magherafelt
Probate District:	Londonderry
Area:	21,755 acres
Population in 1831:	14,091
Topography:	Situated in the valley of the Moyola River this parish is bounded to the north and west by the Sperrin Mountains.
Towns:	Maghera (population of 1,154 in 1831)
Landowners in 1837:	The Mercers', Vintners', Salters' and Drapers' Companies and the See of Derry.

RECORD SOURCES

Tithe:	1828
Griffith's Valuation:	1859
Census:	1663 (Hearth Rolls), 1740 (Protestant Householders), 1796 (Flax Lists), 1831, 1901 and 1911.

CHURCH REGISTERS

Church of Ireland:	Baptisms from 1785; marriages from 1798 and burials from 1809. Now joined with Killelagh.
Presbyterian:	Culnady
	Curran. United with Castledawson in 1906.
	Maghera – Baptisms and marriages from 1843 and burials 1861-1865.
Roman Catholic:	Part Maghera – Baptisms and marriages from 1841 and burials 1848-1888
	Part Lavey – Baptisms 1837-1839 and from 1852; marriages 1837-1839 and from 1852 and burials 1837-1839 and from 1868.
Methodist:	Maghera (in Magherafelt Circuit) – Baptisms from 1825

GRAVEYARDS AND TOWNLANDS WHERE FOUND IN 1859:

Roman Catholic:	Brewery Lane, Maghera and Main Street, Maghera Fallagloon

TOP TEN SURNAMES IN 1859 (in descending order):

1 Convery; 2= Bradley and O'Neill; 4 Henry; 5 Lagan; 6 Clarke; 7 Wilson; 8 Anderson; 9= Connor and Donnelly

MAGHERAFELT CIVIL PARISH

County:	Londonderry
Barony:	Loughinsholin
Diocese:	Armagh
Poor Law Union:	Magherafelt
Probate District:	Londonderry

Area:	8,291 acres
Population in 1831:	7,275
Topography:	Situated on the River Moyola this parish is generally fertile.
Towns:	Magherafelt (population of 1,436 in 1831)
	Castledawson (population of 674 in 1831)
Landowners in 1837:	The Salters' Company

RECORD SOURCES

Tithe:	1828
Griffith's Valuation:	1859
Census:	1663 (Hearth Rolls), 1740 (Protestant Householders), 1766 (Religious Census), 1796 (Flax Lists), 1831, 1901 and 1911.

CHURCH REGISTERS

Church of Ireland:	Baptisms 1718-1793 and from 1799; marriages from 1720 and burials 1716-1771 and from 1799.
	Castledawson (Diocese of Derry) – Baptisms and burials from 1846
Presbyterian:	1st Magherafelt – Baptisms 1703-1706, 1771-1780, 1813-1861 and marriages 1769-1782
	Union Road, Magherafelt – United with Lecumpher in 1926.
	Castledawson – Baptisms and marriages from 1805. United with Curran in 1906.
Roman Catholic:	Magherafelt – Baptisms and marriages from 1834
Methodist:	Castledawson – Baptisms from 1825
	Magherafelt – Baptisms from 1825

GRAVEYARDS AND TOWNLANDS WHERE FOUND IN 1859:

	Churchwell Street, Magherafelt and Townparks of Magehrafelt
Church of Ireland:	Castledawson Street, Magherafelt
Presbyterian:	Main Street, Castledawson and Meeting House Street, Magherafelt

TOP TEN SURNAMES IN 1859 (in descending order):

1 Johnson; 2 Brown; 3 Stewart; 4 Keenan; 5 Bradley; 6= Keane and Lennox; 8 Steele; 9 Duncan; 10 Bell

TAMLAGHT CIVIL PARISH

County:	Londonderry and Tyrone
Barony:	Loughinsholin in County Derry
	Dungannon Upper in County Tyrone
Diocese:	Armagh
Poor Law Union:	Magherafelt in County Derry
	Cookstown in County Tyrone
Probate District:	Londonderry in County Derry
	Armagh in County Tyrone
Area:	2,506 acres in County Derry
	2,447 acres in County Tyrone
Population in 1831:	2,854
Topography:	A fertile parish, in the valley of the Ballinderry River, situated between the Sperrin Mountains and Lough Neagh. This parish was created in 1783 by separating six townlands from Ballyclog Parish, County Tyrone and six townlands form Ballinderry Parish, County Derry.
Villages:	Coagh (population of 393 in 1831)

RECORD SOURCES

Tithe:	1827
Griffith's Valuation:	1859 (Derry), 1860 (Tyrone)
Census:	1663 (Hearth Rolls), 1740 (Protestant Householders), 1796 (Flax Lists), 1831, 1901 and 1911.

CHURCH REGISTERS

Church of Ireland:	Baptisms from 1801 (gap 1808-1820); marriages from 1829 and burials from 1834. Now joined with Ballinderry and Arboe.
Presbyterian:	Coagh – Baptisms from 1839. United with Ballygoney in 1931.
Roman Catholic:	Arboe – Baptisms and marriages from 1837
	Coagh – Baptisms and marriages from 1865

GRAVEYARDS AND TOWNLANDS WHERE FOUND IN 1860:

Church of Ireland:	Tamlaght (Derry)
Presbyterian:	Coagh (Tyrone)

TOP TEN SURNAMES IN 1860 (in descending order):

1= Cooke and Shaw; 3= Ferguson and Hamilton; 5 Nesbitt; 6 Costelloe; 7= Cowan, Devlin and Jordan; 10 Doherty

TAMLAGHT FINLAGAN CIVIL PARISH

County:	Londonderry
Barony:	Keenaght
Diocese:	Derry
Poor Law Union:	NewtownLimavady
Probate District:	Londonderry
Area:	16,467 acres
Population in 1831:	7,356
Topography:	Bounded by the River Roe to the east this parish, which lies two miles west of the town of Limavady, is very fertile in its northern part but mountainous in its southern portion.
Villages:	Ballykelly (population of 290 in 1831)
Landowners in 1837:	The eastern portion, which was originally granted to Sir Thomas Phillips by James I, belonged to the freehold estate of NewtownLimavady while the Fishmongers' Company owned the western part. A small portion was also owned by the See of Derry.

RECORD SOURCES:

Tithe:	1826
Griffith's Valuation:	1858
Census:	1663 (Hearth Rolls), 1740 (Protestant Householders), 1796 (Flax Lists), 1831, 1901 and 1911.

CHURCH REGISTERS

Church of Ireland:	Baptisms, marriages and burials from 1796.
Presbyterian:	Ballykelly – Baptisms 1699-1709, 1805-1819 and from 1826 and marriages 1699-1740, 1805-1811 and from 1845.
Roman Catholic:	Limavady – Baptisms from 1855; marriages from 1856 and burials 1859-1869.

GRAVEYARDS AND TOWNLANDS WHERE FOUND IN 1858:

	Ballykelly and Mulkeeragh
Church of Ireland:	Drumond
Roman Catholic:	Oghill

TOP TEN SURNAMES IN 1858 (in descending order):

1 Moore; 2 Kane; 3= Connor and Miller; 5 McLoughlin; 6 Morrison; 7 Martin; 8 Thompson; 9 Mullen; 10= Doherty and Sherrard

TAMLAGHT O'CRILLY CIVIL PARISH

County:	Londonderry
Barony:	Part Coleraine and part Loughinsholin
Diocese:	Derry
Poor Law Union:	Ballymoney and Magherafelt
Probate District:	Londonderry
Area:	16,835 acres
Population in 1831:	10,070
Topography:	Situated in the Bann Valley this parish, which lies three miles northwest of the town of Portglenone, is bounded by the mountains of north Derry.
Villages:	Tamlaght, Glenone and Innisrush
Landowners in 1837:	The Mercers' Company, Vintners' Company and the See of Derry.

RECORD SOURCES

Tithe:	1833
Griffith's Valuation:	1859
Census:	1663 (Hearth Rolls), 1740 (Protestant Householders), 1796 (Flax Lists), 1831, 1901 and 1911.

CHURCH REGISTERS

Church of Ireland:	Tamlaght O'Crilly Upper – Pre-1870 none
	Tamlaght O'Crilly Lower – Pre-1870 none
	Tamlaght O'Crilly Lower and Upper parishes are now a united parish.
Presbyterian:	Boveedy – Baptisms from 1841; marriages from 1842 and burials 1849-1863. United with 2nd Kilrea in 1923.
	Churchtown – Baptisms from 1840 and marriages from 1839.
Roman Catholic:	Greenlough – Baptisms from 1845 and marriages from 1846. Greenlough was originally part of Kilrea Parish.
Reformed Presbyterian:	Drimbolg

GRAVEYARDS AND TOWNLANDS WHERE FOUND IN 1859:

Church of Ireland:	Drumnacanon and Tyanee
Presbyterian:	Bovedy and Drumard
Roman Catholic:	Drumagarner and Inishrush

TOP TEN SURNAMES IN 1859 (in descending order):

1 Mulholland; 2 Kane; 3 McCahy; 4 Henry; 5 McErlane; 6 Mihill; 7 O'Neill; 8= Cassidy and Dimond; 10 Mullen

TAMLAGHTARD CIVIL PARISH

County:	Londonderry
Barony:	Keenaght
Diocese:	Derry
Poor Law Union:	NewtownLimavady
Probate District:	Londonderry
Area:	13,129 acres
Population in 1831:	3,607
Topography:	Bounded by Lough Foyle on the west, by the Atlantic Ocean to the north, by the River Roe to the south and by the mountains of Binevenagh (1,260 feet) to the east this parish lies four miles northeast of the town of Limavady.

RECORD SOURCES:

Tithe:	1826
Griffith's Valuation:	1858
Census:	1663 (Hearth Rolls), 1740 (Protestant Householders), 1796 (Flax Lists), 1831, 1901 and 1911.

CHURCH REGISTERS

Church of Ireland:	Baptisms 1747-1764, 1817-1818, 1831-1839 and from 1844; Marriages 1747-1753, 1820-1829, 1832-1834 and from 1845; and Burials 1747-1776, 1824-1829, 1831-1840 and from 1844. Now joined with Aghanloo.
Presbyterian:	Magilligan – Baptisms and marriages from 1814. Census of Congregation c. 1850.
Roman Catholic:	Magilligan – Baptisms and marriages from 1833 and burials 1863-1880.

GRAVEYARDS AND TOWNLANDS WHERE FOUND IN 1858:

Church of Ireland:	Duncrun
Roman Catholic:	Tamlaght

TOP TEN SURNAMES IN 1858 (in descending order):

1 Doherty; 2 McLoughlin; 3 Kelly; 4 Kane; 5 Mullen; 6 Begley; 7= Conn and Sweeny; 9= Butcher, Campbell and Somers

TEMPLEMORE CIVIL PARISH

County:	Londonderry
Barony:	Northwest Liberties of Londonderry
Diocese:	Derry
Poor Law Union:	Londonderry
Probate District:	Londonderry
Area:	12,772 acres
Population in 1831:	19,620
Topography:	Bounded by the River Foyle and Lough Foyle on the east and by County Donegal in the west.
Towns:	Londonderry (population of 10,130 in 1831)
Landowners in 1837:	The Irish Society was the principal landholder

RECORD SOURCES

Tithe:	Not dated. The tithe entries are listed against the Deanery of Derry which also includes entries for the County Donegal parishes of Burt, Inch and Muff. Until 1809 the Parish of Templemore included the parishes of Burt, Inch and Muff.
Griffith's Valuation:	1858
Census:	1663 (Hearth Rolls), 1740 (Protestant Householders), 1796 (Flax Lists), 1831, 1901 and 1911.

CHURCH REGISTERS

Church of Ireland:	St Columbs' Cathedral – Baptisms, marriages and burials from 1642. St Augustines' – Pre-1870 none Christ Church – Baptisms from 1855 Culmore – Baptisms from 1867 and marriages from 1868
Presbyterian:	1st Derry – Baptisms and marriages from 1815 2nd Derry (Strand) – Baptisms from 1847 3rd Derry (Gt James Street) – Baptisms from 1838 and marriages from 1837 4th Derry (Carlisle Road) – Baptisms from 1838 and marriages from 1839. Ballyarnett – Baptisms and marriages from 1848
Roman Catholic:	Long Tower (St Columba's) – Baptisms 1823-1826 and from 1833 and marriages 1823-1826, 1835-1837 and from 1841. St Eugene's – Baptisms and marriages from 1873
Methodist:	Londonderry (Carlisle Road) – Baptisms from 1820
Reformed Presbyterian:	Londonderry (Clarendon Street)
Congregational:	Londonderry
Independent:	at Bridge Street, Londonderry in 1858

GRAVEYARDS AND TOWNLANDS WHERE FOUND IN 1858:

Church of Ireland:	Ballymagowan, Culmore, Killea and Lonemoor Street, Meeting House Row and St Columb's Court
Presbyterian:	Shantallow
Roman Catholic:	Long Tower

TOP TEN SURNAMES IN 1858 (in descending order):
1 Doherty; 2 McLaughlin; 3 Gallagher; 4 Bradley; 5 O'Donnell; 6 Quigley; 7 McDaid; 8 Campbell; 9= McDermott and Thompson

TERMONEENY CIVIL PARISH

County:	Londonderry
Barony:	Loughinsholin
Diocese:	Derry
Poor Law Union:	Magherafelt
Probate District:	Londonderry
Area:	4,801 acres
Population in 1831:	2,551
Topography:	Bounded in the north by the Moyola River this parish lies two miles southeast of the town of Maghera.
Landowners in 1837:	The Vintners' Company and the See of Derry.

RECORD SOURCES

Tithe:	1828
Griffith's Valuation:	1859
Census:	1663 (Hearth Rolls), 1740 (Protestant Householders), 1796 (Flax Lists), 1831, 1901 and 1911.

CHURCH REGISTERS

Church of Ireland:	Baptisms 1821-1839 and from 1846; marriages 1821-1838 and burials 1833, 1846 and from 1855. Now joined with Desertmartin.
Presbyterian:	Knockloughrim – United with Bellaghy in 1928
Roman Catholic:	Lavey – Baptisms 1837-1839 and from 1852; marriages 1837-1839 and from 1852 and burials 1837-1839 and from 1868.

GRAVEYARDS AND TOWNLANDS WHERE FOUND IN 1859:

Mullagh

TOP TEN SURNAMES IN 1859 (in descending order):

1 Paul; 2 Shivers; 3= Elliott, Hunter and Sheils; 6 Arrell; 7= Brennan and Scullion; 9= Bradley, Brown, McCracken, Murphy and Porter

www.ingramcontent.com/pod-product-compliance
Lightning Source LLC
Chambersburg PA
CBHW072202160426
43197CB00012B/2489